Soulmate DOG

My Journey Home with Luna's Guiding Wisdom

SHAWNA MARIE FISCHER

SOULMATE DOG
My Journey Home with Luna's Guiding Wisdom

ISBN: 978-0-578-36551-0

Author Photo and Cover Photo
by Team Wyla's Mom

Cover Design and Interior Design
by Transcendent Publishing
www.transcendentpublishing.com

Printed in the United States of America.

*Dedicated to Luna—my soulmate dog—
who is forever in my heart.*

Peace, Love, And Paws!!

Stewart Marie Gunther

Contents

"Shawna Marie Fischer has done an outstanding job sharing how unconditional love and healing changed her life in amazing ways, via this beautiful soul, Luna. In *Soulmate Dog: My Journey Home with Luna's Guiding Wisdom* she touches on the joys of connection, inspiration and presence that truly only our four-legged friends can offer us. This story will touch your heart and call to mind those that have changed your life for the better, especially those in the animal kingdom."

— **Sunny Dawn Johnston**, Best-Selling Author of
Invoking the Archangels and *The Love Never Ends*

INTRODUCTION

In 2005 I was fortunate to adopt a yellow lab named Luna. This book is about the years I spent with her and the inspiration, peace and love she brought into my life. Luna helped bring me back home to the *me* I'm truly destined to be.

Have you ever felt lost, like you don't even fit in your own skin and body? This feeling of not being at home within myself was something that I experienced from early childhood. As an adult, I chalked this up to being adopted, even though my parents were loving and supportive and open around the facts of my adoption. It also didn't help that I have always been sensitive and able to hone in and pick up on things that others were not tuned into. For many years I was at a loss as to what to do with my intuitive gifts. Lonely and unfulfilled, I made one poor relationship choice after another.

Until I decided to adopt Luna, a beautiful yellow lab with wisdom in her eyes. When I first saw Luna, I felt a strong familiarity wash over me, like the comfort which comes when hanging out with an old friend one hasn't seen in a long time. It was as though she was the part of my heart I was missing. Our connection and communication, instant and strong, caught me off guard, causing me to wonder. Did we know each other?

Soulmate Dog: My Journey Home with Luna's Guiding Wisdom is the story of how in loving and connecting with Luna, I healed from two abusive relationships and embraced my sensitivities and my intuitive gift, namely that of being an animal communicator. Luna opened me up to possibilities I hadn't even allowed myself to consider. I fulfilled a dream of mine and moved to Seattle. When circumstances changed for me, Luna taught me how to be gentle with myself and accept that change is a part of life. If it wasn't for Luna, I wouldn't have been open to having life-changing surgery for endometriosis. With Luna, I got to deeply examine my feelings around being adopted.

Luna passed in 2017. But this was not the end of my time with her. Instead, the most profound part of our journey together began. I felt Luna's presence in an even deeper way in my life, and with her guidance, I intuitively knew to continue the search for my biological father. I found out that he, too, had passed. My journey with Luna, one of connection and transformative loss, helped me deal with the fact that I never got to meet my father on this physical plane. When I heard his name for the first time and saw his picture, I felt a deep sense of peace and completion. I had come full circle. I was finally at home within myself.

I wrote *Soulmate Dog: My Journey Home with Luna's Guiding Wisdom* to inspire pet owners to deepen the relationships they have with their animal companions and to share what I have learned about animal communication. My hope is to inspire readers to have the courage to pursue their passions, to shine a light for all of those who are adopted and searching for the home within, and to offer comfort and hope to those who are struggling to free themselves from abusive relationships. The intention of this book is for it to be a source of inner strength and faith to readers. *Soulmate Dog: My Journey Home with Luna's Guiding Wisdom* will remind readers that love and connection are what help us find our way to the home within ourselves.

Chapter One

MEETING LUNA

I was not always the best about realizing and knowing my worth when it came to relationships, especially my intimate ones. Until Luna came into my world, I had been in a marriage that lacked mutual respect and friendship. Upon leaving that relationship, I gave myself some time to enjoy the single life and being on my own. I loved spending time with my friends. One night I went out and met who I thought was a great catch—oh my, this was not the case! Ultimately, I ended up losing more of myself and my self-worth. The time came for me to take a stand and be on my own again. How was I to do that? I had my loving Jovie cat, who was always ready to share her sweetness with me. I wanted extra companionship to fill my heart and mind, and I craved the company of a dog in my life again. I questioned if I was worthy of more. Luna opened me up to the fact that I was, and more than I realized. With Luna's help, I started taking the necessary steps to venture out on my own again.

When I first met Luna, I was in the midst of a breakup. I was leaving an abusive relationship and had not lived by myself in about four years. I had suffered verbal and physical abuse and was in a relationship with an alcoholic. I had walked on eggshells, always attempting to adjust my behavior to my ex-boyfriend's moods. I was working at a local Humane Society and on the lookout for a dog to join Jovie and me in our new home. So, I set out on a mission to find the perfect dog! My co-worker, Ava, happened to be fostering a mama dog and her eight puppies. Knowing, as everyone did, that I wanted a dog, she suggested I adopt the mama dog. Always having an open mind, I thought: *Okay, why not?* About two weeks later, the fateful day arrived for me to meet the mama dog, and there stood the most beautiful yellow lab with wisdom in her eyes. She was not as I pictured; she was so much more. When I saw her, I felt a strong familiarity wash over me like the comfort that comes when hanging out with an old friend you haven't seen in a long time. I knew from the moment I saw the mama dog that she was meant to be in my life. Our connection and communication, instant and strong, caught me off guard, causing me to wonder: *Did we know each other?* Nonetheless, through this, she showed me when you know it's right, it's right. It is a matter of just not questioning your knowing.

Ava kindly cared for the mama dog until Jovie and I were settled in our new home. During this time, my excitement from knowing she would soon be part of my every day kept me going. Luna's work with me began with giving me something to look forward to as I embarked out on my own. I was not making much money and was not sure how I could support myself, let alone add another mouth to feed to the mix. Did I have all the things a new dog would want? Was I prepared to offer her everything she deserved? Did I have the time she needed me to have to spend with her? What if, for some reason, it did not work out? What if the connection I thought we had was not what I thought it was? Was I ready to bring a dog into my life?

All these thoughts stemmed from being with my ex-boyfriend. He made me think I was crazy, causing me to doubt myself with his constant emotional, verbal, and sometimes even physical abuse. Sure, I had all these doubts as to how I was going to afford a dog and offer her all she deserved, but when any of those thoughts came to mind, so did a picture of the mama dog embodying faith and unconditional love, and bringing me comfort and strength. She helped me to find the light within myself. This was the start of her sharing her wisdom with me and helping me regain my self-worth. Little did I know this was also the start of one of the most amazing relationships of my life. She was far from perfect, just like me, and I loved her. This was the beginning of my healing with my soulmate dog. With her by my side, I found the courage to start reflecting on my life's journey.

Feelings of joy and anxiety streamed through my mind in the days and hours before bringing Luna home. A little over a month had passed, and the time for me to bring mama dog home was finally here. I met up with Ava and brought mama dog home. It was time to show her a new place to live and introduce her to Jovie. The introduction went as well as can be expected, with them giving each other a sniff-down. They acclimated quite quickly, learning to tolerate and respect each other. Next came the time to uncover her name, which took some time. I thought to myself: *What would be the perfect name for her? Did she have a name she was used to? Did she want a new name?* Many names crossed through my mind; none of them really seemed to stick. I had been talking to some co-workers about this struggle, as I wanted one which would suit her perfectly. We all tossed some names around, and finally, the right one came up. It was Luna—a perfect name to fit her soul. And, as it turned out, Luna could not have been a better name for her, as I soon discovered that Luna was not much of a barker, but more of a howler. Her howl was magnificent, as though she was singing her name.

Since it had been several years since I had lived with a dog, there was a lot to remember about having one around. Luna helped me to recall those things very quickly. She reminded me of the importance of putting food away quickly. One night, I decided to make a cheese pizza. I took the pizza out of the oven with the cheese all melted and perfect. I took two pieces and put them on a plate, and went to enjoy the deliciousness that awaited me. When I was done, I went back to the kitchen to put the pizza away. To my dismay, it no longer sat delightfully oozing cheesy goodness on the cutting board. I thought to myself: *Did I put the pizza away already?* Suddenly my focus shifted to Luna. I gazed at her just lying there and looking at me, wondering what she was so intently focused on. Why did she have such a devious, happy look on her face? Then, it occurred to me—Luna had devoured the rest of my pizza! Luna was quite pleased with herself, so all I could do was smile at her contentment and the situation. All was forgiven as Luna was just being resourceful and taking advantage of indulging in a treat that was filled with cheesy goodness. Luna reminded me about not holding back, to enjoy the deliciousness in life when it appeared, and let it truly soak in.

One of our first adventures was Luna modeling a hat I had purchased but never wore. Turns out, she didn't like the way it looked, as I found parts of the brim chewed up in a nice pile. It was in a new shape that was obviously more pleasing and appealing to Luna. After she had redesigned it, she lost interest in the hat as well. Luna taught me that if you are not going to make use of something, maybe it is time to find a new use for it or get rid of it. So, this hat ended up being one with the trash can, as it was not appealing to me anymore.

Luna and I were acclimating quite well together. That was until Luna discovered that I toss and turn a lot when I sleep. One night I woke to find myself flipping to my left with my right foot lifted in the air and almost kicking Luna in the head. I heard a loud, snarling growl! Ferociousness had awakened us both! It was a standoff of sorts for a moment or two as we looked at each other. No words were spoken out loud—it was true heart-to-heart communication. Telepathic communication had begun by me letting Luna know that I sometimes toss and turn in my sleep. She communicated back, "Thanks for letting me know." Her having this new awareness helped her cope. This reminded me of the connection and awareness between us that was always there whether we were sleeping or awake. We were finally able to go back to sleep, having a new understanding of bed boundaries.

Luna and I enjoyed many comforts, such as taking time to just be in the moment, with no plans for the day other than to simply see what comes to be. I recall a rainy day, and chocolate chip cookies sounded perfect, so I decided it was time to get those cookies made. Luna laid down nonchalantly as I prepared them to go in the oven. To avoid boredom while waiting for the cookies to bake, I stepped into the next room to peruse the internet. When the timer went off, I returned to discover an empty counter, and all the nice, hot, gooey chocolate chip cookies were gone! There was no question in my mind Luna had relished in the tastiness of those cookies. This was a lesson in taking the time to enjoy the moment right in front of you as they go by so quickly—in a flash, really. However, for me, panic set in and my mind raced! Luna had just eaten chocolate! Would she need to be rushed to the ER Vet? I looked at Luna, and a sense of calm came over me. She had a way to calm my mind and soul, helping me take a moment to breathe, and gently relaxing into the present time. After I regrouped, I called the ER Vet. They asked me what kind of chocolate she ate, how much she ate, and how much she weighed. Luckily, it was only a small amount! In that moment, Luna taught me that sometimes we must relax and let go of worry. The good news is she ended up being okay, and what a relief that was. Luna immediately started teaching me to lighten up.

Luna had to wait to get spayed after I adopted her. She had an extreme case of mastitis, from her being a mama dog to eight puppies. Her nipples were hanging down like a cow's udder. It looked like the puppies had sucked her nipples to death and then had a game of tug of war with them. This was a serious medical condition that sometimes happens with lactating female dogs. Her spay had to be delayed to get this more under control. When the time came for her spay, I dropped her off at the vet. When the time finally came to pick her up, she staggered out from the back. She was very out of it and was not really herself. The vet staff had mentioned it was due to the fact she was still coming out of the anesthesia. So, homeward bound we went. Luckily, I was able to spend the rest of the day and the following day with my sweet girl. Dinnertime had arrived, but Luna was not at all interested in food. She must have been hungry from fasting from surgery. I thought to myself, *What am I to do?* I scavenged through the pantry and fridge. Was there something there I would be able to feed her? Then it struck me—eggs were the perfect option. Now, how to cook them? There were so many choices that would be easier for her to digest. Then it came to me— scrambled. So scrambled eggs it would be. After they were scrambled up, I blew on them as I did not want Luna to burn her tongue. She patiently watched as I did this. Finally, they were ready to be put in her bowl. She put her nose up and showed no interest in them at all. Knowing she had to eat, I had one more trick up my sleeve. I put a handful of eggs in my hand. That did the trick and Luna ate them right from my hand. Whew, what a relief it was! The next day she came back around and was more herself. Luna reminded me we nurture the ones we love and do what it takes to help them.

Luna and I on our first trip to the Oregon Coast together.

Chapter Two

LEARNING MY WORTH

I continued to struggle with my finances during my first year with Luna. I was working over 50 hours per week and struggling with balancing work and home life. I was barely making a livable wage. I started off making $8.00 an hour and moved up to making $8.53 at the end of my time working at the Humane Society. The benefit that offset my wage was the fact that my health insurance was provided at no cost to me. Too exhausted to cook and lacking the creativity to make budget-friendly meals, I often ate cereal for dinner.

In the evening, Luna would comfort me by lying with me on the couch. She would look in my eyes when she felt my mood and energy shift. Her gaze was one of unconditional love and trust. Whenever I gazed back at her, I felt my energy shift. I felt a responsibility for her, and I sensed she felt a responsibility for me, too. As I struggled to find my self-worth, Luna slowly started to help me discover it within myself. I have not always been the best at being kind and gentle with myself, and I often put myself down with negative self-talk. I never really felt like I fit in as a child, and I was picked on and bullied. This experience of being different has always been a part of me.

Realizing that I had to make a change to look after Luna and myself, I found a job as a server. This was scary at first, as I would only be working about 20-25 hours per week. It ended up that I made more money and had more time for myself and Luna. It was hard for me at first to realize I was worthy of this. Luna helped me to understand that I was, in fact, worthy of this and so much more. This was all a huge part of healing from the abusive relationship I had been in. I had also never really known what it was like to find the home within oneself, since I had been adopted, and I was always searching for my place in the world. Luna helped me to embrace that, and we found that together.

Going to the coast was always a favorite pastime for Luna and me—one of our first times at the coast was going "coast hopping." We drove on the beach in Long Beach, Washington, where that is legal. Luna and I enjoyed the nice, fresh, salty air and how fun it was to be able to drive on the beach. There was even a spot where stood a tall bridge, with a fascinating trail that led to a little tide pool of water. The temptation to go explore struck, so down the trail we went. It was quite steep; hesitation overcame Luna and me. I took a step, then Luna followed suit. With each step I took, she looked at me to ensure I was okay. Finally, we made it to the bottom, and, thankfully, there was water for Luna to take a quick, restful soak in. We took some time to relish in the splendidness before us. Thank goodness we knew what to expect with the walk back up.

One of our coast trips had a great start—the ending was not so great. The first part of the day, taking a jaunt on the beach, was perfection. Wading through the water and then taking time to explore some shops was fabulous. There happened to be a hot spot casino nearby, and by a stroke of luck, we made it there in time for the breakfast buffet. As it turned out, it was not so lucky at all. About two hours later, stomach upset kicked in, and I began vomiting. We started home, as I was supposed to go to a Candlebox concert that night, and it was about a two-hour drive. Thankfully, there were many places to pull off the road as the uncontrollable vomiting set in. Luna ended up being content with one of the spots, which happened to have a small, shallow creek that she couldn't help but jump in. It was as though she was saying, "See, Mama, I distract you to make you feel better!" Finally, we made it home and were able to settle in. I was hoping to be able to go see Candlebox; however, the food poisoning really kicked in with other plans. Instead of going to see Candlebox, it was a trip to the ER to get fluids and to get some electrolytes on board. Luna kept a watchful eye on me. Within a couple of days, I felt much better. In this situation, Luna reminded me that all we can do is make the best out of situations that arise.

Luna and leashes—she did well with them—that is, if she was walking and doing what *she* wanted to do. Luna was full of determination when she had her mind set on something. She did not back down, always finding a way to do what she wanted. One day we were at the vet, and while Luna was finishing up in the back, I was at the front getting my bill settled. Luna must have known it was soon time to come home, because a couple of minutes later, I heard what sounded like one of the vet techs trying to wrangle a dog. Not a minute later, Luna came trotting up with a slip lead on because she had chewed her leash in half and made a break for it. Just a little reminder to break free from what is holding you back.

Another time Luna had been boarding at a kennel, and they had left her leash hanging on the kennel. Totally harmless, right? Easy to have it right there for walks. Well, Luna did not like her leash there, it must have been in her way or tormenting her just by hanging there, and surely it was not going to clip itself to her to go for a walk. Well, that leash, too, ended up being in pieces. Luna knew what she wanted and went for it— a reminder to go for the things that you want and that are waiting for that which you are resisting. The good thing is, the company I had purchased the leashes from had a chew guarantee and would replace any chewed-up leashes. Wow, they must have had my dog in mind. What was fun was a new pattern that could be used as the new replacement leash, and Luna and I always enjoyed picking out a new one. It is always fun to break out of a rut and try new things.

Luna had many hobbies, some she enjoyed more than others. One of her most favorite pastimes was speed reading. First, she would take a book that interested her from the bookcase. She would then decide if she liked the book—if not, the book would end up with pages torn out of it and shredded all over the floor. She only took one book at a time and really focused on that one book. This is something I really learned from, as I have a lot of books, and sometimes, I end up reading more than one at a time, which can be a good and bad thing. Luna taught me sometimes we need to focus on one thing to really dig into it. Other times it can be good to juggle our focus to stay well-balanced, as long as we stay on course. Luna had many speed reading experiences. Some were on their own, and others were combined with other incidents.

One of the most memorable ones, I call the Great Escape. While I was at work, Luna was always in her kennel. She had one of the extra large plastic crates with nuts and bolts that attached the top part of the crate to the bottom. I had the kennel put together with just the top part attached to the bottom part of the kennel, and they attached fine without the nuts and bolts, so I felt no need to use them. Well, I felt differently when I came home from an errand to find the kennel unattached and diarrhea everywhere. It was as though a painter had just painted Luna's kennel and my carpet, and it was a big mess! Well, after her diarrhea explosion came to an end, she must have got bored and decided it was now time to read. Pieces of a book intermingled with diarrhea—oh boy, what a mess it was. The cleanup began. Two important lessons came out of all of this. One was that it was time to put the nuts and bolts on the kennel! The other lesson was to enjoy treats in moderation, as Luna had enjoyed a larger-than-normal holiday treat that day. Luckily, it did not take long for her to start feeling better.

Luna was my protector; she always looked out for me. One night, we were on our last walk. We took the path we always did, except on this particular night, I felt called to walk in the opposite direction. Luna was always a little cautious of men. On our walk, there was a man in his late 20s who passed by us. Luna suddenly let out a low grumble-growl and slanted her eyes in his direction. This was way out of character for her. He walked past us very quickly. Luna guided us home right after this. I was so grateful for her alertness and her protection over us. We made it back home safely, and I remember how grateful I was that we were safe and that we happened to walk in the opposite direction that night. It is so important to listen to nudges of guidance that come our way and to have an awareness of all that surrounds us.

Luna had a remarkably interesting hiding place when she wanted to have a moment to herself. I had an antique wood table with a glass top that I had knick-knacks and crystals in. One day I was looking for Luna and found her under the table. It had always amazed me how she could get out from under it without lifting the table. Who knows, maybe she was giving herself a healing session with the crystals I had in there? The lesson she taught me from this is, even if we are in a tight spot where it seems there is no way out, it is about finding the way out.

Working at the Humane Society gave me insight into the importance of fostering. So how could I not help with this? Cats and kittens were always in need of fosters. I happened to have a big enough bathroom to keep any cat or kittens separate from my fur babies. Ready I was for my first foster. It was a set of kittens. There were many fosters to follow. Another set of kittens, then a litter of kittens with their mom. I ended up fostering the mom another time. I really wanted to adopt her; unfortunately, I was not able to. The good news is that she was back at the Humane Society after my last time fostering her. I was working, and someone had inquired about her. Luckily, I happened to be working in adoptions that day, making it possible for me to talk to the potential adopter, who turned out to be a perfect match. That made my heart happy.

Then there were the adult cats with upper respiratory infections that I fostered because they needed to get out of the stress of being at the shelter. It was always really rewarding to see them make a full recovery. This was especially true with one cat that had an extreme upper respiratory infection. The vet had let me know when I picked her up that there was a chance she would not make it. I was determined to get this cat well again, and that I did, as she made a full recovery. Luna always stood by as I would administer medications to my foster cats and would remind me to keep putting in that energy of determination. The vet was quite surprised when I brought her back to the shelter for adoption. This was no surprise to Luna as she always had faith in me.

It was always fun to have the fosters around. Leo especially enjoyed it as he took some of what he had learned from Luna and let the foster kittens try to nurse on him. A nurturer and teacher he was. Even though there was no possibility of milk from nursing him, it was comfort from the suckling. Leo knew this and was happy to accommodate. Luna, on the other hand, tolerated the foster kittens and cats. She did this as she knew how much they needed help and how much it meant to me. To her, it reflected how she and I needed each other. The shelter ended up needing a foster for a sweet young lab mix named Pebbles. The foster was just needed for one night. Of course, having a love for labs, how was I to say no? She settled right in, making herself at home on my bed. Luna was not too fond of this. Oh boy, did she make this known by claiming her spot on the bed. She was very gentle about it using her sharp, keen motherly instinct. She was claiming her territory and letting it be known she appreciated being the only dog in the house. Once it was established that Luna was in charge, they both settled in for the night. It was a relief for Luna when Pebbles left the next day to go to her new home.

Luna and Leo in one of their first moments together.

Chapter Three

AWAKENING TO CONNECTION

Luna and Jovie were together for almost a year. Then suddenly, Jovie became ill. It happened rather quickly. Jovie had not been herself. She hid in the dark and ate less than usual; even her bright, black, plentiful coat appeared lackluster and thin. I fed her special canned food, even heating it to coax her, but without success. She continued showing no interest and began to refuse to eat. I decided to treat her by speaking to her gently while attempting to hand feed her as my other hand administered Reiki's soothing touch. Unfortunately, Jovie responded minimally. The next step in her healing journey necessitated a visit to the vet. Upon examination, the vet discovered Jovie was unable to maintain her body heat and suggested many tests with a bleak outlook at best.

It turned out to be an incredibly sad day. Here I had taken Jovie to one vet with no clear answers as to what was going on with her. After talking it over with my precious girl, we determined a second opinion was warranted. I, luckily, have an aunt who worked as a veterinary technician. She said, "Bring her right away," so off we went on the 40-minute drive to

Newberg. During that time, I comforted Jovie by talking to her. We arrived at the hospital, ready for our next step.

The consultation resulted in multiple tests, as well as Jovie being treated with a heating disc in an attempt to return her body temperature to normal. After many, long tenuous hours, the time to discuss Jovie's condition and prognosis had arrived. The results shed no light, and she refused to stay on the heating disc. So, the time to make a hard decision was upon me. I checked in with Jovie, and she let me know it was time for her to make her exit from the physical world. Looking into her eyes, I saw she was between dimensions of time and space. Her actions ultimately communicated the same message—it was Jovie's time to transition. I stayed by her side until she crossed over, helping her by transferring the energy of love and peace.

It was a hard drive home without Jovie. Tears overcame me and it seemed like forever before I finally made it home. Luna could feel the sadness in me, and there was an emptiness in the house without Jovie's physical presence. Upon arriving home, Luna gave me comfort, and she had the knowledge that Jovie had passed on. It was so hard to sleep that night. The time on the clock kept passing by, hour by hour, with no sleep. It was 3:00 a.m., and I needed to get some rest. Luckily, there was a gas station and market two minutes away from my apartment. So, off I went to get some Tylenol PM. Thank goodness it did the trick, and I was finally able to get some much-needed sleep.

Jovie left an indelible mark on my heart. We had been together since she was three months old, and now to let go of her after three short years had passed proved profound. Jovie taught me graciousness with her presence and knowledge. Approximately a week later, I went to my dentist's appointment, and as I left, I noticed this little white kitten in a car parked just outside the door. The attraction was immediate! Something so familiar and intriguing about this kitten simply grabbed me. Suddenly, I had to use the restroom and ran back inside, all the while hearing the kitten meowing loudly in my head while the anxiety in me rose. I hurried back to the car as quickly as I could and felt instantaneous relief to see the kitten was still there. Feeling the same from him, I decided to wait for the people attached to the car. They finally returned! I asked if this was their kitten and they told me how he and his sister had been dumped outside their house. Additionally, they explained how they'd brought him with them on this day to protect him from his sister's continuous attacks. I now know a bigger reason for our meeting existed.

I shared with them Jovie's story, and they promised their rescue kitten to me. A week later, we met, and I took him home, my new six-week-old kitten. It felt too soon, but in the depth of my heart, I knew it was right. I asked Jovie for a sign showing me it was okay. On the way home, I saw a sleek, black cat, reminiscent of Jovie, eating tall grass in a far-off meadow. This cat stared intently at me from a distance, and a whole-hearted energy exchange happened between us. I knew right then I had Jovie's blessing.

Luna's happiness abounded when I brought home this new little bundle of ever-flowing energy and love. They instantly bonded as if they had known each other for years. Luna helped me figure out who this kitten was by their instant connection. She obviously recognized his essence of being straight away. Of course, why would Luna not recognize him when he came back into my life? I had yet to connect the dots. I thought to name our new little kitten, Spirit, but it was not feeling quite right. Upon asking him his name, he answered: Leo. It resonated! He responded! That was it! Leo. He was a funny little kitty in the many ways he acted like a dog. For example, the way he would play with Luna, lay next to me like a dog, and dig in the litter box as if he was digging holes in the dirt. Leo even preferred dog food and would love it if I had let him—he begged worse than Luna!

The more time I spent with Leo, the more I felt I had known him for years. I had a dog many years prior named Rex, a beautiful red and white Aussie mix, who always acted like a cat. He would lay up behind me on the couch wrapped around my neck; he was extraordinarily agile, and jumped just like a cat. He would even catch Frisbees by pouncing on them with his front paws. Rex was always bonded with me, and I missed him very much when he left my life, even though I knew his presence was always abounding in my life. Although he was no longer with me in body, he was always with me in spirit. Then, the dots began to connect! Both chose kingly names. How fitting that he chooses the name Leo in this life. They were the same colors; Rex had been an Aussie mix of white and red, and Leo, a distinguished flame point Siamese mix. A dog acting like a cat and a cat acting like a dog. Could it be possible that Leo and Rex were the same soul? Then, I looked at him and knew—there was no denying it! Leo and Rex were one and the same.

I was humbled that Rex had decided to grace me again with his presence in that present time. I was overwhelmed that he had found me, and I was impressed at how connected we still were. As Rex, he had taught me to respect and honor my journey as well as to find my path within myself. As Leo, he took those lessons to deeper levels.

About three months after Leo arrived, Linnus Magnus came into my life. Now, when Linnus came into the picture, it was not an instant connection, more of a tolerance for each other that they all had. Luna knew Linnus would be a good friend and companion for Leo. Linnus was a reminder for me that sometimes what comes your way is needed even if it is not what you had planned. I was not planning to get another cat when Linnus came into our lives. It was New Year's Day, and here was Linnus, a young kitten roaming in the apartment complex where I was living. There was a busy street nearby that he was getting close to, so, without a thought, I picked him up and brought him into my bathroom to ensure his safety. He had tags and a microchip number, enabling me to find his people. I called them to let them know I had found him. The woman let me know that it was her husband's cat, and they were planning to make him an outside cat because there was stress with their current cat, and he was also pooping on their son's bed. I found out he was only about three months old. Not sure what came over me, I told her that I would be happy to take him in if they didn't want him. She said she would ask her husband and get back to me. I heard back, and it was a go for me to keep him. Yay, they agreed—it was so natural. The first thing I did was change his name to Linnus, which he helped me come up with—it fit him perfectly. Leo and Linnus Magnus clicked right away and ended up having a great kinship. Luna and Linnus, on the other hand, had a relationship of tolerance and respect. Luna had the same rapport with him she had with Jovie—respect my space, and I will respect yours. Linnus Magnus's energy and personality traits were similar to Jovie's. I know she sent him to me to enhance my life and bring me comfort, and he completed our family. Linnus Magnus, Luna, and Leo impacted my life by bringing me constant joy and inspiration.

There were times where they would all lay together. This reminded me to treasure small precious moments, and it is not about how many of these moments we have; it is about the quality of these moments. There were many wonderful moments with Linnus. These experiences taught me many things—the joy and honor to give to animals the gifts and lessons they freely bestow upon us, unconditional love and living life to the fullest, respectively. When one engages in this energy exchange, it results in peace and comfort for all involved, and sometimes, their offerings and teachings occur in different time elements and frames.

Luna was a natural when it came to nurturing Leo. Leo, being only about two months old, still had a desire for a mothering touch. Luna was more than happy to take on this role. Luna loved her Leo. She became Leo's second mom. She was always so patient with him; letting him try to nurse on her, as she knew the comfort that would bring him. Luna had an amazing ability and knowingness of when nurturing was needed for her Leo and for me.

There were many ways she took on this role. One of Leo's favorites was how Luna would let him nurse on her. Although there was no milk, it was the suckling that brought Leo much comfort and happiness. Luna always kept a close watchful eye on her Leo kitten. This was the start of a great friendship between them. Seeing Luna and Leo's connection awakened such peace, love, and comfort within me. They both shared a love of food, and, incidentally enough, they also loved sharing food with each other. Who would have thought? They each had their favorite foods and likes. Cheese was always a big hit. As soon as the wrapper would crinkle open, out of nowhere, they both would appear—with their ears up and alert, "Cheese, cheese, where's my cheese?" They waited happily for their disbursements.

They loved it when the mood to bake struck me as that meant their help would be needed. They especially loved it when I baked cookies, even more so when the cookies had been beaten perfectly. That meant it was time to get the mixer beaters cleaned, and who better to help than Leo and Luna as they licked them spotless, making it easy to throw them in the dishwasher. They reminded me of the importance of lending a helping lick and paw. Luna and Leo loved to play the "paw-paw game" with each other. Where Leo would paw at her, and they would bounce all about having fun. Their favorite pastime was soaking in each other's love by lying together.

Luna always reminded me of the importance of keeping her in the loop with my comings and goings so she would know what the day looked like for her. She was not happy with me when the timeline that occurred did not match the timeline I gave her, and it ended up being different. Boy, oh boy, let it be known that if no timeline was given, well, that would for sure not be tolerated by Luna either.

One example of this comes to mind. I went on a two-week trip, which happened to be the longest I had been away from Luna. So, you would think I would have remembered the importance of communicating the timeline with her. As always, when getting ready for a big trip, last-minute packing and details ended up stacking up and time ended up passing by quickly. I dropped Luna off at her favorite kennel, where she loved the people and the kennel. I bid my farewell, letting her know I would see her again soon. I got so wrapped up in my trip, that I was lacking in my check-ins with Luna as much as she would have liked. The time came for me to go pick up my girl, and I was so excited, I even got a speeding ticket on the way. I first had to make a quick pit stop to get one of my tires fixed, and I wanted to get that done as quickly as I could. Thank goodness the fixing of the tire was not a long ordeal.

The time had come to see my girl. She gave me her usual happy greeting with a look of, "Shame on you, Shawna, for leaving me so long and not checking in on me as much as you should have!" She gave me the cold shoulder treatment, or should I say cold paw treatment. We stopped by a friend's house before the long drive back home. Luna was not happy with either this stop or having to share my attention. She wanted to get back home. To make up with Luna, I decided to make a quick stop at McDonald's on the way home. She was happy to enjoy the plain cheeseburger I had treated her to. This was the start of her forgiving me. By the time we were back home, Luna was happy again and so relieved to be back home with me and her Leo and Linnus. She reminded me to allow myself time to unwrap from being wrapped up, and take time to connect with the constant wrappings in my life.

Luna and Linnus had quite an interesting rapport. Sometimes they would have a moment of admiration for each other, which was always a shock, as those moments would just come out of the blue. I learned to not question those moments, instead, to just enjoy them as they came, as they were rare moments. In one of their non-admiration moments, Linnus was lying right where Luna wanted to walk. It was like watching an old western to see who was going to draw their gun first. Finally, Linnus gave Luna a free pass by him. The relief that came over her was priceless. During these moments, they reminded me that every relationship is different, and it doesn't have to be perfect. It's a matter of embracing all the quirks and differences in each relationship.

Luna had quite the forgiving soul—always quickly forgiving me for my humanness. Oh, so grateful for this I was as she helped me to let go of feeling bad. A couple of times that she did this still stick in my mind. Luna always loved food and mealtime. She never hounded me to feed her when it was time to eat. Well, that was until one day when it came time for Luna's dinner, and it occurred to me that I had forgotten to give her a morning meal. So that night, she got some extra food and a big apology from me. Thank goodness she was quick to forgive me and not hold on to the fact that she had missed her breakfast.

There was one day I had training out of town that was going to add a few extra hours to Luna's normal day at home while I was at work. This was a day where forgiveness was from both of us. I had given an extra key to Luna's foster mom, so she could come and take Luna out for a walk and a potty break. Well, as it turns out, I should have done a key check, because this key was not the correct key to open the front door. When she came to let Luna out, the key did not work, and she could hear Luna from the other side of the door. Unfortunately, the apartment complex I lived at was not able to offer help at that moment. So, of course, I had forgiven Luna when she had an accident in the house—what else was she supposed to do? I gave her extra love and an extra-long walk when I got home. Luna reminded me that life happens and that I am human, and it is better to not hang on to what hangs us up and to just move beyond it.

Most dogs bark when they want to be heard. Well, Luna had her own way of making her wants and desires known. She insisted on howling her desires. Boy, oh boy, was she matter of fact and oh so persistent with her howling. If I was taking too long to get ready for an anticipated trip to the dog park, she would howl and stomp her two front feet with much vigor. The dog park was her place of freedom and fun—to smell, to run, and be out in the fresh air. She would also howl if there was something she wanted me to see or know. The insistence of her howl also let me know which of her howlings to pay attention to. She had a way of bringing insights to me, such as at bedtime when I was winding down for the night. She would give up and go put herself to bed if she thought I was taking too long. It was as though she was saying, "Enough with your dilly-dallying—it is time to go to bed and get some rest to get replenished for the next day." I tried my best to pay attention when she brought this to my awareness. She reminded me in these times to take the time to listen, and, not just listen, but follow through as well.

Witnessing all of this connection awakened a deep desire within me for more. I started reaching out to old friends and making new ones. I was moving out of isolation, which is typical of those in abusive relationships. This was also the start of my discovery of animal communication. This ability has been with me from childhood, but now the moments of awareness and insight were coming rapid-fire. There have been several instances of this occurring with the animal companions of friends and even strangers. When I acknowledged this gift of mine, I also started to learn how to connect to myself.

When I first opened myself up to animal communication, it was perfectly timed. You see, I have had many jobs that have never fulfilled me. That was until my animal communication work came into play. You might be wondering how that happened. I was at a monthly gathering led by one of my friends. After the gathering, my friend and I were outside talking near our cars. She mentioned to me how she and her boyfriend had just acquired a new cat. Then, out of the blue, I started to describe the cat's size, colorings, and personality—not fully realizing what I was doing. My friend looked at me in awe and full amazement. She asked me if I had ever thought about being an animal communicator. I thought to myself: *Hmm, I wonder what animal communication is all about?* I decided to find out more about animal communication and to explore it further. From there, I read all I could about the subject and started taking some classes. Luna gave me the courage to start putting myself out there more and embracing this newfound skill that was always a part of me. This opening up expanded my heart in ways I never imagined and filled me with joy.

I remember my first animal communication session. Before I met the dog, I had a picture of her in my mind, which happened to be exactly what she looked like when I met her. In one of my first experiences with animal communication, I was at a stoplight, and in the car next to me, there was a dog about the size of a Chihuahua in the passenger's lap. The passenger kept moving about, shifting where the dog was lying in their lap. I could feel the frustration and dizziness it was causing this dog. As I gazed at the dog and tuned in, this dog gave me a deep stare as to say, "No kidding, this is annoying; I wish they would just stay still." There was also a thought of, "Wow, you can hear me!"

Another time I was leaving a workshop, about to cross the street, and a 40-ish-looking guy was about to cross the street in the opposite direction. His dog would not let him cross that way. He ended up crossing the street in my direction. I, of course, ended up complimenting the dog. The guy mentioned how strange it was that his dog insisted on crossing the street in the opposite way he wanted him to. I mentioned the fact that I am an animal communicator. He then said something about the dog's diet, and I was able to offer some insights from the dog regarding that. They both ended up being incredibly grateful for this chance meeting.

One time I happened to be on my way to an in-person animal communication session. My GPS was going crazy and kept re-routing me and getting me turned around. This made me a few minutes late to the session when I usually like to arrive early to prepare before meeting with my clients. I took a moment to reflect on what was going on with this, as this had never happened before with my GPS. Then it came to me how frustrated I was about this whole escapade. It finally clicked—it was related to some frustration the dog I was about to meet with was going through. I was able to bring this up in the session and bring some solutions to the table to help the dog with this.

While helping a client find their lost terrier mix, I was in contact with the owner about what I was picking up from her dog and where she was. I was able to give her insights that helped bring her dog back home. This dog had mentioned to me that something was wrong with her front left leg. All of my communications had been done over the phone with this client; however, when it came time for an in-person session to help with the other pets in the household, the terrier mix came up to me and lifted her leg to show me where she had been injured.

Another time I had a session for a cat. The cat was mentioning something about Cheetos and wanting Cheeto treats. I remember thinking to myself, "Cheeto treats…what? How was that even possible?" But the cat was very insistent about this. Finally, I mentioned it during the session, and the people told me about a treat in the shape of a Cheeto that had a crunchy texture. They mentioned the cat had not had that treat in a while, as they were out of it, and it happened to be one of the cat's favorite treats.

One day while walking with Luna in the apartment complex we lived in, there was a dead bird in the road. There was also a crow that was moving the bird little by little. I kept thinking: *Come on, crow, you can do it; move it, move it.* Strategizing in my head of how I was going to move this bird. The crow was clearly tuning into my thoughts and looking at me. It was as though the crow wanted me to be even more clear and patient. So more clear and patient I became and then, voila, the crow picked up the bird and went off in flight.

I share these stories with you to show the different ways animals are always communicating with us, and that sometimes the way they communicate is not always what it seems to be. The more we tune in and explore animal communication, the more open we can be to hearing what animals want to communicate with us.

Luna snuggled with Leo and Linnus.
Linnus giving Leo a hug with his paw.
They made a heart with this love snuggle.

Chapter Four

LOOKING FOR HOME

I was in the middle of a move, and as with any move, my place was a mess with boxes scattered about the living room floor and piles of papers and odds and ends that still needed to be packed. I had not even started work on the kitchen, and now I was out of boxes and tape. So off to Safeway I went for more supplies. I would only be gone for about an hour, and I figured Luna would be fine out of her kennel. Well, that might not have been the best idea.

I came home to find out that Luna had been busy unpacking! Two boxes of books were strewn across the floor. Not only had Luna unpacked, but she also had a fun speed-reading session with one of my favorite books, *Meditations of a Parish Priest*. There it was in pieces in front of me. I bent down and gathered the pages—some of them still salvageable. What made Luna chew this book and scatter other books all over the floor? Did she not like the way it smelled? Did she not like the way it looked? I stood there, perplexed, trying to figure out what was going on.

Luna gave me a look that said, "Well, I was just trying to help, and these boxes happened to be in my way." I knew there was more going on with her. This book had belonged to my maternal grandfather. Some of the pages had been dog-eared and highlighted by him. To be able to open the book and flip to one of its many inspiring pages had given me comfort over the years. I turned to Luna, who was all curled up and enjoying a nice little nap after her grand book adventure.

It struck me that this was our first move together. With Luna being a rescue, this must have brought up something inside her, possibly some memories and heartache. I did not know much about her history other than the fact that she came in from a rural area as a stray with eight young puppies that were still nursing. Didn't she know how much I loved her? I realized I was so wrapped up in the move and carrying frantic energy around that I had not taken the time to let Luna know what was going on. Picking up on my energy, she was frantic by default.

I breathed deep, reminding myself to slow down. I also needed to remind Luna of how much I loved her and that, of course, she was going with me. Our animal companions are so sensitive to what is going on around them and in the lives of their humans. By chewing the book, Luna had reminded me that she picked up on everything around her, whether I realized it or not. I kneeled toward her with my face to her face and gave her some gentle pats and love. I held her face in my hand. "Oh, Luna, you're my good girl, and I love you so much," I said.

I put the torn pages and chewed cover in a bag. It could be repaired in some fashion, or I could search for another copy. Luna, however, was irreplaceable. Then, I went on my way, sorting through my kitchen items. I was amazed to find things in there I had not used in quite some time. Since my mind was not in the right space to get rid of those things—some dishes and platters from my prior marriage—I packed them anyway. It's funny how sometimes we can have a hard time letting go of something that is no longer serving us. Once that was done, I started to go through and purge items in my food cupboards. Looking back, I know I was in a stagnant place in my life; part of me knew this move would bring much-needed healing. I kept on with the packing even though I was uncertain what was going to be showing up for the future.

For the past several months, I had struggled to find consistent income. I thought I was in a secure position with my job as a server at a local restaurant until one day, I came in, and one of my coworkers pulled me aside before the start of my shift. She told me that I no longer worked there and did not give much detail as to why. This was right after the engine blew up in my old car, and I had just bought a new car with more expensive car payments. How was I going to afford to live, let alone pay my new car payment? Through all this, Luna was my rock.

On my daily walks with Luna through the apartment complex we lived in and the surrounding neighborhood, I forgot about my worries. Just being in her presence lifted my spirits; she had a way of bringing me to a neutral space of calm clarity. On most days, we took the same route, but Luna always showed me something new to bask in as though it was the first time we'd walked that way. Through this, she opened me up to her way of being in the world. Luna was at peace at the moment, and the more and more I opened to this peace, the more possibilities she brought to my awareness. Whenever I had an "A-ha light bulb" moment during our walks, Luna gleamed with happiness.

Several job opportunities fell through, and unemployment was insufficient, but during our walks, a dream that I'd had for years started nudging me. What if I searched for employment elsewhere? Seattle, for example. I had always dreamed of moving there. Growing up in Southern California—Long Beach, to be exact—I was always drawn to the ocean and water. I also love rainy days, that crisp fresh rain scent, and the way the rain washes one's soul clean, bringing in new ideas and clarity. I felt a pull to Seattle for this very reason. Since nothing was panning out in Vancouver, Washington, I decided to make the move to my parents' house to save up money for a new life in Seattle. They were incredibly supportive of the idea and bought a little travel trailer for me, Luna, Leo, and Linnus to live in.

My parents arrived bright and early on moving day with their truck and trailer to help me. We loaded up all my belongings and piled up even more stuff to be hauled to the dumpster. I gave away my dining room table and chairs and my bed. I wanted to start with a clean slate. It did not take long to get everything loaded up, but the closer we got to leaving, the more I kept stalling for more time. I had been on my own for several years and was not ready to go back to live with my parents. I procrastinated. I fussed over packing up the final odds and ends. I checked every nook and cranny of my apartment to make sure that there was nothing I had inadvertently left behind. I saw my parents growing frustrated.

They like to get things done and get moving, whereas I like to have time to process my experience. Through all this, Luna waited patiently, making sure she knew where I was. When I dawdled, she looked at me intently and moved her head slightly to signal me gently to keep moving. She helped bring us both comfort. Finally, my apartment was bare. Linnus and Leo were not all that happy to be loaded up in their crates for a long car ride. Crates were for trips to the vet, and it always amazed me how far they could extend their legs to resist being placed inside one. I put their crates side by side, and Luna jumped in and took the rest of the back seat. It was time to hit the road as we had about a five-hour drive ahead of us.

Home? Was I going back home? I felt so displaced and uprooted. I did not know what home actually meant to me. The one place that had always felt like home was where I grew up in Long Beach, California. I had lived there from the time I was about thirteen months old until I was nineteen when my parents retired and moved us from California to Applegate, Oregon. Here I was, this girl who had graduated from high school and was studying audio engineering in the evenings and working full time in the day. It was an exciting time; my life started to feel like my own, and I was discovering more of who Shawna was. Talk about culture shock! Applegate was a rural area, a half-hour from town, and to me, civilization. Four miles down the road, there was a country store with a gas station, café, and post office attached to it. No mall close by, no option of five or more beaches to venture off to. I thought meeting my husband-to-be was an escape from all of this. Oh boy, was that not the case. Instead, during that four-year marriage, I started to lose sight of the Shawna that I had recently been discovering.

Since adopting Luna, I had been questioning the true meaning of *home* and knew it was more than just a house of my own. My parents adopted me when I was thirteen months old. Before that, I had been in two foster homes. I was moved out of the first one after a few months, because my first foster mother did not pick me up as much as she should have and instead left me sitting in a carrier most of the time. This explains some issues I had during childhood as I did not have the nurturing I needed as a baby. I struggled with forming relationships with kids my own age and even had panic attacks. Fortunately, I grew out of those panic attacks by the time I was about five.

Questions around being adopted persisted. Having been adopted, a part of me never felt complete. In nurturing Luna and having her nurture me, I had started to realize that just because my biology was different from my parents, it did not mean I was missing something or was any less of a person. The more time I spent with my soulmate dog, the more she helped me to get in touch with my heart. My passion for animal communication had awakened, and I was ready for my life to open up more. But here I was driving back to my parents' house. I felt as though my life was moving backyards in a downwards spiral. Luna helped me to realize that this was a temporary move and that there was an end goal in place. I was also starting to realize that the home I was longing for was not a place. It was the home within myself.

A decade earlier, when I was in my early twenties, I had hired someone to find my biological mother. Within a month, they contacted me, gave me her name, and told me she was from Ohio. The search was on to find her phone number, to reach out to her. I contacted her ex-husband, and he gave me information about the daughter they had together. I researched phone numbers with her name and started making calls. I had no luck with the first few phone calls and was starting to wonder if I would ever reach her. Finally, I had the right number, and I nervously dialed it. With every ring tone, the anticipation built up inside me. She picked up the phone and confirmed her name. I proceeded to ask her some questions to see if this was, in fact, my birth mother I was talking to. Then I told her I thought I was her birth daughter. There was a little pause in the conversation. It seemed to be a relief for both of us that we had found each other. I had wondered about her, and she had wondered about me.

I had so many questions for her and did not know where to begin. Of course, the perfect place to start was by getting to know about her family. Did she have other kids? Did she have any siblings? Were her parents alive? I learned she had a daughter who was raised by her ex-husband and that she had a daughter after me, who she had raised. She had recently come back in contact with the daughter who was raised by her ex-husband. I also found out she has two sisters and three brothers, and that one of her brothers and one of her sisters lived near her, and one of her brothers had passed away. Her mom lived near her, as did her dad, but she did not see too much of him. I proceeded to let her know about my adoptive parents and my life.

It ended up being an easy, naturally-flowing conversation, and we made plans for another call. Wow, what a discovery it was to find out who she was! Soon we were discussing the possibility of me coming to meet her in person, as well as some other people in my biological family. I was married at the time, and my husband was somewhat supportive of me going on the adventure back to Ohio, even though I do not think he understood what this meant to me as he was not adopted.

A few months later, I boarded a flight out of Eugene, Oregon, about two and half hours from where I lived. So many thoughts ran through my mind. Here I was about to take a five-hour flight to meet strangers and stay with the woman who carried me for nine months. What if they did not receive me well? What if we had nothing to talk about or had nothing in common? Would I look like them? Would I have similarities to them? Would we have a deep connection? Would meeting them help me to have a deeper understanding of myself?

The longest part of the flight was right before we landed in Dayton, Ohio, when all my nerves set in. Once through the gate, I saw her off in the distance. As I got closer and I was face to face with her, I sighed with relief. We hugged each other, and it was nice, but it was not what I anticipated it to be. I thought that I would be overcome with emotion, that it was going to be some earthshattering experience like the encounter one might see on one of those adoption reunion shows. Instead, I had a neutral feeling of "Okay, now I know what she looks like face to face."

I stayed at my biological mother's house for about a week, meeting my two biological half-sisters, my biological maternal grandmother, one of my biological mother's brothers, and one of her sisters. I also met some biological cousins. Odd things clicked into place. I remember I went on a grocery store run with my biological mother and her sister. We were in the meat aisle, and I remember my biological aunt picking up some meat and inspecting it thoroughly and even smelling it. I took a step back in surprise. I did this when I went shopping. I had always wondered where I got this as my mom never did it.

On my flight back home, I thought that, sure, it had been an interesting visit, but it did not solve everything. I did not feel the deep connection I had anticipated and that I longed for. They were nice people, but I still felt a part of me was missing. My biological mother did not know who my biological father was. Would finding out who he was complete me? And how would I even do so? I'm grateful to my biological mother for knowing what was best for her and for me and for being a part of bringing me into the world.

After that visit, I had renewed gratitude for the mom and dad who did raise me. I knew they were brought to my life for a reason. They were the parents I needed. My biological parents were just the vessel that brought me to the family I was meant to be with. They needed me, wanted me, and it was the same for me with them.

We pulled into my parents' driveway at about 6:00 p.m. Eager to see what there was to explore and smell, Luna scrambled out of the car. I took her for a quick little walk and potty break, and then it was time to bring Leo and Linnus into the trailer. I had to carry them in one at a time. Linnus was a bigger cat, and I wanted to make sure I ensured their safety as we were out in the country on ten acres, and it was about to get dark. They were not too sure what to think about this new place, other than the fact they were incredibly happy to get out of their carriers. This was not the accommodations we were all used to. It was a 26-foot travel trailer that was not very wide. On entering, you saw a couch, then a small dinette area with a small kitchen right beside it. Then, a short walk led to a shower with a small bathroom across from it, and a few feet beyond that was a small closet. Nestled in the back were two twin beds. It was awfully close quarters for two cats, a 60-pound dog, and me. The good thing was the view from the window in the dinette area. I sat down and looked out at the densely forested area where birds were flitting about in the twilight. This made it hard to look for work, as being in this nature was so peaceful. Taking Luna on walks around the property and to the creek brought me much peace, as did spending time sitting with her on the front porch, basking in all the crisp fresh country air.

A lot had changed since I had been that nineteen-year-old who felt so isolated in the country. Now I appreciated all the wildlife I saw at my parents' property—deer, raccoons, squirrels, lizards, and all kinds of different birds. The more time I spent walking in the woods, the more I sensed the comfort all these creatures felt being in nature. Their home was many different places, not just one place, and it truly lived within each of them. Being able to witness that was very powerful. Luna enjoyed all the smells she would encounter from all the wildlife.

One of my favorite things to do while there was to shake apples from the apple tree for the deer. I would roll the apples towards them and they knew the wonderful bounty that awaited them to feast on. I also enjoyed watching the lizards; they have a way of doing pushups as they sunbathe. These observations helped me to deepen my connection with the animals, and they reminded me how easy it is to communicate with them when we let go of distractions. One day I discovered a lizard in my parents' house behind the TV. Of course, I had to help this lizard get back outside and into its natural habitat. I could not just pick up this lizard. So, what was I to do? The "A-ha moment" hit me when I noticed a stack of DVDs right by me. All I needed to do was communicate with the lizard to get on top of one of the DVDs, so I could help it back outside to be reunited with its lizard family. I put the DVD right in front of the lizard, and it happily hopped on for a little magic DVD ride back outside.

Luna was a city dog and not used to all the creatures in the country. One day, while I was out in the front yard with Luna enjoying all the beauty around us, I spotted several deer on the other side of the fence, safe from Luna. That was until my mom needed to move the sprinkler in the front yard to give the deer some fresh water. She opened the gate ever so slightly, and Luna made a break for it. The chase was on. Across the road into the forest, Luna ran. I chased after her, my heart racing, my mind frantic with worry. I tripped and fell, trying to catch her. Thankfully, my mom decided to follow the road to the right and then up into the woods. She was quick on her feet and remained calm and in the moment. I was absolutely beside myself, coming down from the woods not having my Luna with me. Then, all of a sudden, in the distance, I saw Luna walking with my mom down the road—as if nothing had happened and she had not charged off on an adventure. I was overjoyed with happiness at the sight of my girl.

Over time, Luna and the deer grew more accustomed to each other and came to a mutual understanding of each other's existence. Luna would sit calmly on the porch watching them, and the deer, in turn, had figured out they would not be chased, so they calmly foraged, with an occasional glance in her direction. Mutual respect was had by all.

Luna also had her first experience with wild turkeys at my parents' home. When they came wandering through the trees, she stared at them and sat perfectly still, her nose pointed at them as though she was calculating a plan. Her focus was steady and alert on the turkeys' every move. I was blown away by her focus—nothing, I mean nothing, distracted her until the turkeys dispersed and flew away. She reminded me of how hard it can be for me to keep my focus and how easy it can be if we remain present and in the moment.

Luna and my mom had a great relationship. My dad and Luna, on the other hand, were constantly testing each other. Luna was used to the comforts of being inside. My dad had put in a lot of hard work into building an outdoor kennel for her, piecing it together with metal roofing and chicken wire. Luna was not sure about this contraption and why she had to stay in it when clearly there was so much more to explore. She had quite the adventure shredding and ripping different parts of it to pieces. My dad realized that he needed to make some adjustments to the kennel. Out came the bicycle bungee cords to help secure the kennel. Strong and durable, right? Not according to Luna. To my dad's amazement, she found a way to gnaw through them. Well, let's just say the challenge was on. Out came the stronger wire to cinch up the spots where Luna was trying to break through. She still had a way to get out. Then my dad got the "wire of all wires," and sure enough, that did the trick. Their relationship ended up evening out. That was until my dad decided it was time to break out the weed eater, and oh, how Luna would not stand for that! She barked and barked, overpowering the sound of the weed eater every time it came out. So, we did our best to keep her inside when weed eating needed to be done.

There were many great memories and times Luna and I shared together at my parents' house. Luna loved to sit on the front porch with me and just enjoy the nice crisp fresh country air. Well, that was when the air was fresh. Back in my more inexperienced days of pet products, I thought I had found a perfect natural flea treatment for Luna. The scent, I remember, sounded delightful. Delightful it was not. On this afternoon, Luna and I happened to be sitting on the front porch with my Mom and Dad while they enjoyed their afternoon coffee. I remembered the flea treatment and thought it would be a perfect time to put it on Luna. I do not remember it smelling too bad. Luna, on the other hand, was trying to figure out where that god-awful smell was coming from. She sniffed her butt and, well, it wasn't coming from there—how was that even possible? Luna persisted to try to figure out where the smell was coming from, but it followed her as she ran away from herself and as she ran back and forth on the deck. This flea treatment ended up being entertainment for my mom, my dad, and me. Luna was trying to escape her whole body, jumping about with no jump rope in sight, running back and forth down the porch to escape this awful smell. Finally, I was able to catch her and rinse some of this not-so-wonderful smelling flea treatment off her.

Usually, the time on the porch was for sitting and just enjoying the beautiful scenery and waving at the occasional car that would go by. The front porch and yard were some of Luna's favorite places there, aside from the forest with the tall trees and the creek. She loved the creek, and her favorite thing to do there was to reflect. As the water would pass by, she would walk into the water, plop down, and enjoy a fresh drink of water.

Even though I was now staying with my parents, I still had bills to pay. I filled out application after application for office jobs and restaurant jobs. I was also actively searching for a job that involved working with animals on a day-to-day basis. When I saw that a nearby veterinary hospital was looking for an assistant, I headed over there with my resume and a cover letter. They interviewed me right on the spot. It seemed to flow so organically, and later that day, they called and offered me the position. Most of the staff I worked with were lovely, but I did not connect with the office manager, who was my boss.

When I told her about my interest in animal communication work—I was hoping she would see how beneficial this could be in a veterinary hospital—she said I shouldn't tell anyone else at the office about this as they would think I was weird. Weird? Talking to animals seems like the most natural thing to me. Two weeks later, I got a call on my day off from the office manager—they were letting me go, as my position was no longer needed. Soon after that, I got hired at a local Applebee's restaurant. What a blessing it was, as I was making full-time wages, only working about twenty-five hours per week, and I had a flexible schedule where I could pick up extra hours as needed or get extra time off. I was able to start paying off my bills and saving money to move to Seattle.

During this time with my parents, I also had the opportunity to explore what I wanted to be doing with my life, and I enrolled in my first animal communication class with Marta Williams held in Novato, California. After learning about animal communication and how it works, we practiced with other students in the class. We were instructed to tune into our partner's animal and write down the impressions that came to us from the animal. I was partnered with a woman who had a horse. As I studied the grainy photo, a *knowing* of this beautiful animal came rushing to my mind. Thoughts, words, and imagines came so quickly I could barely write them all down. Her horse wanted more treats. He liked rubbing his face against her hand and loved it when she spoke to him. He loved to run. He was a serious animal and proud, and it was important to him that I knew I was not looking at the best photo of him. Once we were done tuning into our partner's animal, we shared what we had picked up on. I was so nervous. What if I picked up nothing that was right? What if none of it made sense to her? Thankfully almost all of it made sense to her, and after that, I was excited about some more practice exercises. At the end of the day, I was struck by how easily the knowing had come to me. This was a way of listening and tuning in that made me feel deep with purpose.

The class was held at a community center, and for the second part of the class, we went outside to commune with nature. There were plenty of trees around and planters filled with beautiful flowers and bushes, abuzz with bees, butterflies, and other insects. We were instructed to go to where we were drawn and write down the thoughts that came to our mind as we stood by a flower, tree, bush or insect. It brought me much peace to be outside, tuning into nature. A sense of calm filled every part of me.

A few months later, I traveled to Novato again for another class with Marta Williams, *Finding Lost Animals*. We learned how to tune into an animal that is lost and how to deliver messages from them to aid in locating them. We also learned different things a lost animal might be going through. One exercise involved remote viewing, and we practiced with one of Marta's cats. We saw through the cat's eyes, imagining we were the animal and were able to pick up on what was around us in full detail. I remember picking up on the kitchen curtains with the ruffled edges and how they were tied back on each side of the window. Doing remote viewing was fascinating. It felt almost like detective work. I had a mystery to solve, and the more I tuned in, the more I learned. At this point, I had no idea the huge impact animal communication could make, not only for animals, but also for the people in their lives.

I spent a lot of time reflecting on how I was going to practice more animal communication. I knew I was not quite ready to fully dive into the richness of this world and seek out clients. That would come with my move to Seattle. The time at my parents' house gave me the space to have more awareness come into my life and to work on not compromising myself. I stayed there for a year and a half and was able to pay off some debt and get caught up on some past due bills and collections accounts. It felt so good to have some of this financial strain lifted from me, and I felt excited for the journey ahead.

Luna at Marymoor Dog Park in Redmond, Washington.

(Photography by Team Wyla's Mom)

Chapter Five

HEART CALLINGS

I had always dreamed of living in Seattle, and the time was coming for that dream to become a reality. I had gathered more self-love and embraced my passion for inspiring people to connect in deeper ways with the animals in their lives. I was ready to commit to my path of being an animal communicator, but I had a rocky start. Fast forward a year and a half, and the time for living in Seattle had come to be. Finally, I had enough money to make the move. The only thing that was missing was a job up there. So, I started to search and apply for jobs. I applied for so many jobs in the area, and finally, my due diligence paid off. I landed a job at the Seattle Humane Society as an Admissions Advisor. They wanted me to start work as soon as I could. I was overjoyed and scared at the same moment, as now what I wanted had finally come to be.

In my time with my parents, I did somewhat grasp the deeper meaning of home, and I somehow thought moving to Seattle would fulfill that quest and need. My role at the Humane Society consisted of cleaning cat cages and feeding cats in the morning, and when we opened, I would take in incoming pets. I thought it was going to be the perfect fit, which it was for a period of time, and the good thing was, it got me to Seattle.

So, the time came to move, and I thought I had found a great apartment. Looking a little further, I found one that was better priced and thought it would be perfect. My parents and I, along with Luna, Leo, and Linnus, were prepared for moving day. When we arrived at the apartment, it looked like a run-down motel and was in a bad area. My gut knew I could not follow through with living here. What was I to do? What if, by some off chance, the original apartment I was supposed to move into was still available? I thought to myself, it cannot hurt to call them to see if it was. My mind was filled with anxiety as I picked up the phone to call them. To my relief, the apartment was still available. It would not be ready until the following day. What were we to do? We had a moving truck all loaded and the back of my dad's truck full. We were fortunate enough to get a room for me at the hotel my parents had reservations at for the night. The thing was, they would not be able to take Luna, Leo and Linnus. We had no choice but to sneak Leo and Linnus into the hotel room. Oh boy, what a venture that was. Leo and Linnus were in the same crate, and well, let's just say Linnus was a bigger cat. I was carrying them upstairs, and the crate started to come open. Thankfully, my mom was there to save the day, and I was able to get them safely upstairs and locked in the bathroom. The next day had finally arrived and anticipation set in as it was time to go to my new apartment. I sure hoped my intuition was right, and this place was, in fact, better than the other place. To my relief, it was, and we lived happily in our new home. In the past, worries about my ability to look after myself and my animal companions would have surfaced, but Luna's presence soon grounded me.

Things in Seattle seemed to be going pretty well with my job at the Humane Society. I had even switched to a different role as an operations receptionist in the veterinary area, where they did surgeries for the public, as well as cremation and euthanasia services. It was during that time that more of my animal communication abilities opened up. One example that comes to mind, was a dog who had passed that had come in with a microchip. So, we traced the chip to find the owner to make sure they knew their dog had been found and had passed away. When putting the dog in the freezer, the dog gave me their name, but it was not the one that matched the chip. After contacting the owner, it turned out that was the dog's original name.

Luna helped me to be more open to this ability I had. Our current apartment lease was up, and my commute to work was pretty long—about 40 minutes. I thought of how nice it would be to live closer to work and to be in an area with more nature, as Luna had helped to show me how the stillness of nature helped calm my anxiety and bring me peace. So, with Luna in my mind, I began my search to find that perfect nature spot I so craved that was closer to work—especially after living in the peace and beauty of my parents' property.

I was drawn to a perfect spot that had a beautiful lake nearby, and that was on my drive to many places near me. I felt like this was the place but doubted it would be within my budget. Luna was in my mind as I had this thought and the next thought that came to me was, "You don't know if that's the case until you check it out." So that's exactly what I decided to do, and it turned out they had a great special and a nice apartment with an amazing open view. I soon gave my notice on my current place, and the time came to move, but about one week before moving, I got laid off from my job. So much for moving closer to work. At least I would have that beautiful view. Luckily, I was able to find work that was close by. Luna showed me how being at this peaceful place gave me the ability to calm my mind if I allowed it to do so.

Luna soon became an ambassador for my animal communication work and how I established my business with the creation of my website. I taught my first animal communication class and co-hosted a weekly radio show. I also continued my studies in animal communication with leaders in the field like Amelia Kinkade.

Luna had always been an inspiration for my work with animals. This was especially the case for my animal communication work. She was there cheering me on as I started my animal communication business. Luna helped me to follow my heart regarding my work. She also helped me develop and have more faith in my abilities by reminding me of the importance of it and the faith she had in me. She often helped me with my animal communication sessions and with honing my skills. It was the start of me following the callings of my heart. It was a slow start, then it really got going. So, of course, since Luna had been so pivotal in this, how could she not be my spokes-dog? Of course, all the animals in my life inspired this, but Luna insisted that she get credit when and where credit was due. So, she ended up being on every page of my website. Of course, Leo had his part, too; he preferred to be a silent cheerleader, as did Linnus. Luna was and still is a teacher in the classes I teach about animal communication and she always will be. Luna reminded me clearly and precisely of just this.

One day while we were staying with my parents, I happened to be working on some changes to my website. Luna was in earshot as I was mentioning to my Mom that one day, I would have to find a new spokesdog after Luna passes away. Of course, I was just joking. Suffice it to say, Luna did not find this to be the least bit humorous. She made this protest be known by letting out a howl of disapproval after I had said it. I, of course, swallowed my words and let Luna know that, of course, she will always be my spokesdog. She reminded me that sometimes humor is appropriate, and other times it has no place. This was one of the moments Luna had a look on her face of, "Come on, Shawna, really?" Luna was quite tenacious, and she stuck with tenacity when it was necessary. This was the case in her inspirations for my business.

Luna and I had a favorite dog park when we lived in the Seattle area, Marymoor Dog Park, which was about ten minutes from where we lived. It had everything a dog could want out of a dog park. Places to freely run and smell and water to splash and swim in. Luna loved to run free there and be the natural explorer she was, making sure to take in all the sights and—most importantly—all the smells. She also loved the many options of swimming holes. She did have her favorite spots to jump in for a dip and quick swim. This was a reminder to never lose sight of your most favorite places. There were times she tried a different swimming hole, which was a reminder to embrace your adventurous spirit.

Luna and I had many adventures together at Marymoor park, and being there was one place she did well with other dogs, as she was off-leash and felt less threatened by other dogs. One day we were leaving the dog park for the day, after about an hour of walking around and Luna having a great swim, as well. Just as we were getting close to the exit, we started to walk by an American Eskimo dog. I have to say that American Eskimo dogs have never been my favorite due to some past experiences. As I walked by this dog, a dialogue was going on in my head of how much I was not a fan of these particular dogs. I thought, "Oh great, an American Eskimo dog. I do not like those jerky, unpredictable dogs." I know I should not have passed judgment on this dog, as I know that not all American Eskimos are like the ones I had bad interactions with. Then—bam—suddenly, Luna went up to this dog and snapped at it, which was very out of character for her. It was clear to me she was very aware of the inner dialogue that was going on in my head. Now, to keep to the point, right as this thought passed in my mind, Luna let out a snappy snarl to this dog, and it was game on with the American Eskimo dog striking back, with neither one of them backing down. The person with the other dog was very frantic and started yelling, which I understand was a stressful situation. It was certainly escalating matters. What was I to do? Then I firmly said, "Quiet! Stop!" Once she was quiet, I said very intently and purposely, "Luna, come," and imagined her coming to me. She came right to me, and I quickly put her leash on. Before we left, we made sure both dogs were okay. All was well and good, and they were both completely unscathed from the incident. So, Luna and I continued to the car to make our way back home. This was a reminder that our animals pick up on all our thoughts and are always there to protect us, as I know that was what Luna thought she was doing.

The other important reminder is there are times it is especially important to remain calm in certain situations. As sending out frantic energy only heightens agitation and expands it very rapidly. Instead, taking a step back and breathing before reacting can really help. Also, being firm and to the point limits mixed messages and brings things back to center where the resolution comes with more ease.

Luna and I had a neighbor we would go on walks with in our neighborhood. It was always a fun venture as we never knew what path we were going to take. On this day, we walked on a path by a beautiful wetland area. It was always so peaceful and serene there. To get to and from the wetlands, we had to walk through a neighborhood. I remember seeing a lady jogging and a beautiful black lab-type dog following her. I had my eye on this dog as in my gut, I had a feeling this was not her dog. That was confirmed when the dog appeared again with no sight of that woman. I knew I had to find a way to catch and help this dog. What was I to do? I had no leash with me, and Luna was not all that fond of other dogs when she was on a leash. Thoughts of how to help this dog raced through my mind. Then, all of a sudden, I saw an open garage door. As we got closer to this garage, I noticed someone in the garage. I let them know the predicament I was in, and they had the perfect solution—a rope. Talk about perfect timing! With the rope in hand, I went. The thing was, I knew Luna was not going to be so keen on helping me to get this dog. So luckily, our neighbor friend was with us, and I had her hold Luna while I went to bring the dog to safety. Luna stood guard the whole time, concerned with what I was doing—she was not very happy with me. This was, in part—as it all happened very quickly—because I was not truly clear in communicating with Luna at that moment. Boy, oh, boy, did she remind me of this. She felt better when the neighbor friend took over walking the other dog.

The plan was to take the dog to a nearby veterinary hospital to check for a microchip. As we were walking there, a vehicle slowed down, and as it turned out, this dog was her foster dog who had happened to get loose from her. She was looking for her when she stumbled across us. Talk about perfect timing and trusting that this dog needed help! As it turned out, this dog had an injury she was recovering from. This was a reminder to trust your gut and do the right thing. Luna was happy this dog was back with her foster person so she did not have to share my attention with this other dog.

Luna and I always had fun on our walks together. On one of our walks, we saw a little, newly rescued, white poodle-type dog, who obviously did not want anything to do with Luna. They wanted Luna out of their space, which was a little tricky as I was just making Luna's nightly deposit in the dog waste receptacle. This dog did not want to let Luna and I pass. This little white poodle let out a fierce snarl and growl and was soon in full attack mode. Luna just stood there, standing her ground,

---

standing firm in her spot right in front of me. It was as though Luna had known the stress this dog was under. The people were quick to pick up their newly rescued fur baby. Luna and I were soon on our way back home. Luna reminded me of the gentleness this dog needed at that moment and that more fear would bring unneeded fear to the situation.

Luna was always so great at reminding me to pay attention to what she was communicating to me, which helped ease the line of communication between us. That was, when I remembered to keep the flow of communication open, and boy, did Luna let me know if I was not keeping up with that. As far as not being the biggest fan of other dogs, let's just say Luna tolerated them. There were some dogs she instantly liked, but usually, that was not the case. She liked dogs that were calm and not insistent on her liking them and ones that respected her personal space. She always did much better off-leash when it came to other dogs at the dog park.

There was a dog living next door to us that Luna would love to sit and watch when she was out on the deck. When it came time to be face-to-face with this dog, she was not having any part of it. She liked to put dogs in their place if they were interfering with her boundaries. She wasn't aggressive about it, just to the point, very steadfast, and firm. She was very persnickety around other dogs. There was a handful of dogs that Luna liked in her lifetime. She reminded me in these situations that we don't have to like everyone, but it's especially important that others respect our boundaries.

Luna was never the biggest fan of baths. Well, not the traditional form of baths, that is. She had many different forms of nontraditional baths. She liked rolling in dirt to give herself a little mud bath—a mud spritzer to make sure the fresh dirt smell stayed with her.

Luna loved rolling every chance she got and she was not particular as to what surface she chose to roll around on. One day while walking, Luna discovered a spot I never expected her to—she flipped onto her back and started rolling around on the asphalt in the parking lot by our apartment. She loved the way it would exfoliate her back as she rolled in it really good. She also liked the feel of it as it had course bumps that gave her a nice massage. She always made sure to shake off the grey dirt that lingered on her back. She was not worried if any residue was left; she knew she could always give me a look, and she knew I would brush it off. In this, she reminded me that brushing things off that are bothering us does not have to be as complicated as we make it. She also loved rolling in the grass, soaking up the smooth feel of it as it would take care of any itch she had on her back. She would just dig in and give it her all, swaying back and forth. Well, I guess when you have an itch, you best scratch it out—no matter how rough it may seem, just roll into and with it!

One of her ultimate favorite bath treats was what she thought of as bath beads. She loved the way they would roll over her back, giving her a massage and cleansing her back. Now, these were not the traditional bath beads you and I are used to—these were special "bath beads" made by deer. Yes, you guessed it, good old deer poop it was. She was so proud to roll in them and have their smell radiate through all her fur. In these moments, she reminded me to savor in moments that bring you joy.

Luna was quite the explorer, and she loved sniffing to see what kind of treasures might await her. One day while Luna was outside, she turned to the left and put her nose to work. Within seconds, she had discovered a mole that was not doing well and needed help. She picked up the mole and came to show me what she had found. I asked her to drop it, and she, thank goodness, dropped it out of her mouth. She just looked at the mole and looked at me, letting me know we needed to help this mole. I brought Luna back upstairs. Luckily, I had a little shoebox with a small hand towel to use to put the mole in. There was a veterinary clinic about five minutes from where we lived. So, I gathered up the mole, and off to the vet we went. They could see the distress it was in and helped the mole make its transition out of distress. In this moment, Luna reminded me that we must always look out for our friends who might need help and pay attention to our surroundings.

Luna had many nicknames that all had their own way of coming to be. Some would come as Luna was doing something, while others just came to me by just looking at her. She also had the nickname she came with which, of course, was Mama Dog. Others came in time. Two of the first ones were Luna Bea and Bee. Then came Lunatic, Lunatoon, and Crazytown when she was frolicking about. There was one that was not as glamourous—Luna Tuna. This one I told Luna to keep a secret due to the connotations that came with the name, but apparently, Luna did not like the idea of keeping this secret. I happened to be in the middle of teaching an online animal communication class, and one of the exercises for practice was to have my students tune in and ask Luna about her nicknames. Well, suffice it to say, Luna disclosed her Luna Tuna nickname. I should have been grateful, at least, that she did not include the catchphrase that went with the name. That was a relief. I had to validate that my student got it right. Oh my, how was I to do that? I turned to Luna for guidance, which was, "Well, keep it simple, validate it, why are you making it so complicated?" So, keep it simple, I did, and it went over without a hitch. The important lesson taught to me was, it didn't matter what was or was not going to be thought about this name, it was about giving my students validation of what they picked up on.

Despite the successes I was having, this was still a time of challenge, as my rent had increased dramatically. I'd been in similar situations before, but now I had experience and I knew I could take care of myself and Luna, and that I'd be able to cope with whatever changes life had in store for me. Luna helped me follow my heart, develop more faith in my abilities, as following the callings of my heart helped me to find more purpose in my life.

Luna and I at Marymoor Dog Park in Redmond,
Washington. (Photography by Team Wyla's Mom)

Chapter Six

PAWSITIVE LOVE

Luna taught me to relax and live in the now. In my walks with her, I learned how simply being present can replenish your heart, soul, and mind. Before I adopted Luna, I thought I was relaxing when I was watching TV or playing a game on my phone. But watching TV was often a form of avoidance and contributed to a state of low-level anxiety in my life. With Luna, I finally learned how to relax and work out my anxiety through movement. These days I often see people walking their dogs, cell phone in hand. I was like that, not realizing that the connection I craved was there at the end of the leash, not realizing that simply getting off my phone or switching off the TV boosted my sense of self-love. A person does not bounce back from years of an abusive relationship overnight. My journey to a place of self-confidence took time, and my soulmate dog's strong, grounded and consistent presence in my life helped boost my love for myself and my confidence in social situations. In my work with my clients, I show them how being in nature can nurture and inspire their relationships with themselves and their pets.

Luna often played the role of my wing dog. This happened on many occasions out on walks and at the dog park. She played this role very well and took her responsibility very seriously. which made me happy. We were on one of our afternoon strolls when we happened to stumble across some firemen standing at four different street corners. Oh, my, what a sight to see. Luna for sure picked up on my excitement. She proudly pranced her way to a smoking hot fireman. She smiled and nodded at me, alright, now it is up to you to make your move. She took some nice pets from him. They were out doing their "Fill the Boot" promotion. I did not have any money with me, so we went back home to grab any spare change I happened to have lying around. We made it back just in time, as they were getting ready to wrap up for the day. Luna was lucky enough to get some more pets from the smoking hot fireman. I was not brave enough to make a move, but Luna reminded me sometimes, you just have to make your move, as you never know what you may gain. When the opportunity strikes, go for it!

Oh boy, did Luna love her treats! One of her favorite treats was leftover food on my plate, as she knew it would be hers when I was done with it. Her eyes gleamed, and she swayed back and forth in anticipation of a soon-to-be bite of scrumptiousness that would be coming her way. She waited as patiently as she could. Then, the time came for her feet to dance with anticipation. Her mouth watered as I handed her this tastiness. I quickly learned the importance of holding my hand flat and keeping my fingers out of the line of fire as she snapped whatever tasty treat that was in her sight. She taught me to not hold back in enjoying special treats.

It was my 40th birthday, and who better to spend time with than Luna, and of course, Leo and Linnus? A day of rest and relaxation was in order. I leisurely started off the day in no rush. It was a nice day outside—how could I not soak up the beautifulness of the day? Especially as it was a day for me to enjoy whatever my heart desired. Luna and I had a nearby favorite walking trail, that happened to be right by our apartment, where there was a walking trail in a magnificent wetland area. It was our plan to enjoy some time in this splendor. Off we went, and what a joy it was to be amid all that beauty! We enjoyed a leisurely stroll, breathing in the nice fresh air. There also happened to be a bench overlooking a pond filled with ducks. What a grand sight it was as we took a seat on the bench to be within the beauty that was before us. Time stood still as we basked in the sun. Then it became time to head back home. We ended up relaxing for the rest of the day. Luna taught me in the moments of this day that sometimes it's okay to take time and have a day just for you!

Some dogs love tricks, but that was not the case with Luna. She was not amused with the human fascination with such nonsense. I made many valiant efforts by trying to teach her to shake. She would give me a look like, "Shawna, why must you insist I learn this; what is the point of all of this?" So, I learned to not push her into doing something she had no desire to do. She did, however, like the Eskimo kiss game. Whenever I would leave to go somewhere, Luna and I would exchange Eskimo kisses. This was something she was happy to amuse me with, as she knew it may have seemed silly to some, but it was our little fun time. She taught me in these moments to respect others' boundaries and to be open to the little things that make the ones we love happy.

Luna had a mind of curiosity. She was quite the explorer. One day she found a great treasure of sorts. At least it was for her. She came across a cow head bone underneath my parents' front deck—just sitting there all nice and chewy with the most wonderful aroma and with great chew potential. This had to be explored further to find out if it was as delectable as it appeared to be. Oh boy, it sure must have been, as pieces of white were scattered all over the yard. It was soon to be discovered that the nose was all chewed off this skull—which explained where the white pieces all over the yard came from. Luna reminded me that it is fun to take time to explore the curiosity that calls to you.

Luna had an absolute affinity for water, and she had her favorite water places. Creeks were a special place for Luna. Peace radiated from her as she reflected at the creek. Her favorite creek was the one at my parents' house, as it was nestled in the trees. Sitting radiantly in the flow of the water and her reflection, the water had a way to soothe her soul. Her favorite part of being at the creek was taking a nice plop in the water. She would find a nice spot free of rocks in her way and enjoy a nice soak. The times at the creek were serene. She reminded me of the importance of taking time for silent reflections.

Luna and I enjoyed many walks together—leisurely strolling about, taking in all the sights, smells, and sounds that awaited us. Spring was in the midst, and it could not have been a better day to soak in some fresh air. Dandelions were abounding everywhere we turned. The time to blow a wish was a perfect idea. So, a wish it was. Luna wanted to be a part of all this fun, so she sniffed a dandelion, but she was not about to relish in the absurdity of making a wish. She reminded me that wishes are just an ask away. How could we not take time for a photo op on this splendid day? Luna amused me by posing with a dandelion on her nose. She sat perfectly as she wanted the moment to be exactly right. She taught me about remembering to find amusement and to have fun with it.

As much as Luna loved the water, one would think rain would be no different, but this was not the case at all. Luna was not a fan of the rain. When it came time to go out for a walk and do her business in the rain, she got it taken care of lickity-split! The rain dropping onto her head caused her eyes to squint to better protect herself for the next drop. For me, walking in the rain is invigorating. Luna decided that choosing where the water landed on her was more appealing to her. If she wanted to jump her body in a creek, then it was simply perfect, as she was soaking in the water instead of the water soaking into her! Her favorite part of the rain was coming back inside and getting dried off to get all the pesky rainwater off! Through this she taught me that, just because she liked water, does not mean she enjoyed all aspects of water. So, it's okay to not enjoy all aspects of things we like.

Luna knew that if there was a dog or animal that needed help, her Shawna was going to help. This did not mean, however, that she was going to be happy about it. It was New

Year's Eve and I was working a late serving shift. It was a little after midnight, and there in the middle of the street, stood an older Husky. Of course, I had to help. She had a collar and rabies tag, but not a tag with her owner's information. I tried to coax her into my car with no luck. Then it came to me to take a breath and show her how I was trying to help her. Voila, it worked—she got in my car when I became calmer. There was nowhere to take her due to what time it was, as the local 24-hour vet had no space for her. What was I to do? I had to take her home, but I could not bring her into the house with Luna. So, the only option left was to put her in Luna's outdoor kennel. And to also put out a call to trace her owner through her rabies tag, which was going to be tricky as the next day was New Year's Day. Thankfully, by a stroke of luck, I was able to get in contact with her person. I had to work this day, but luckily, my parents were home to keep an eye on her. The next day I was able to coordinate getting her back home. She was happy to be at home and see her person, and her owner was happy to see her. He had let me know she was not a fan of fireworks, and they had noticed the gate was pushed open. He was grateful I was able to help her and bring her back home. Luna was not happy about this at all and did not appreciate the smell and presence that lurked from another dog being in her kennel. It took her some time to get over this. She was never the same in her kennel after that. So eventually, instead of being in there, she stayed in the front fenced yard. We just had to adjust the back steps on the deck with fencing to keep her in the front yard. She loved this as she could patrol the yard and see when I was coming and going. Every time I would be getting ready to turn into the driveway, she would run back and forth, making a calling sound to me. It was always so refreshing to see how happy she was to see me. It ended up that even though she was not happy about the other dog in her kennel, she was incredibly happy about the new outside arrangements due to this.

Luna took her job of patrolling the yard and property very seriously. This was especially the case during deer season. She kept an eye and ear out for road hunters that would slow their cars down when they spotted deer on the property. Luna and my dad had a special signal where she would alert him when a road hunter was in the midst. She alerted him to cars with hunters out for deer as she would watch the deer nervously run back and forth in front of her outside her fenced yard. She would let out a loud bark, which was only used for this purpose. My dad would then go and pet her on the head, letting her know what a good girl she was to help him run off the hunters. Luna taught me in this that there are special places just for us that we like to keep safe and just for ourselves.

Luna was always willing to make compromises with me. That was, if she was a part of the process. Of course, Luna and I always shared my bed, even though I knew Luna would have preferred having her own bed where she had space to stretch out as much as she wanted. Well, it was about two years before this wish came true for Luna. We were staying in the travel trailer behind my parents' house, and it was like our little oasis on their ten acres. It was a tight fit, but Luna, Leo, and Linnus, and I adapted to it and made it work. I was beyond pleased that Luna was to have her own twin bed all to herself. She did not budge when I tried to get her to lay with me. She enjoyed the spaciousness of her separate bed. There were sometimes when she would appease me and cuddle up close to me. It was as though we were an old married couple. Linnus and Leo mostly slept on the benches at the dinette, and they delighted in the moments I left it open as a bed. So, they had space to lay on top of it and underneath it. I was reminded that it is always important to be open to compromise.

Speaking of compromise, Luna and I had many battles and miscommunications with this regarding her potty training. One would think a two-year-old dog would be completely potty trained. Well, it's a nice thought, but that was not the case with Luna. It took a lot of time, patience, and under-standing to train her to let me know when she needed to go outside and do her business. Crate training did the trick when I was at work or was out running errands, which was only half the battle. Luna was not in her crate at night, so it came time to figure out what to do when I was sleeping. Luna had developed a habit of tippy-toeing very quietly into the living room to do her business when I was asleep. Then finally, it came to me—with Luna's help, of course. She did not want to wake me up. How was I to break this pattern and create a new one letting her know it's okay to wake me up to let me know she needed to go and relieve herself? Solutions raced through my mind. Then, the lightbulb moment flashed into my mind. The perfect solution was to put a chair in front of the door, leaving the door propped open. Perfect for Leo, Linnus and Luna. Leo and Linnus had access to leave and enter the bedroom under the chair. And well, Luna had no choice but to let me know she needed to go out. Now came the time to see how this new arrangement would work. I made sure to be mindful of communicating with Luna about this new plan. She started pacing back and forth making a panting sound, to bring my awareness to her need. I awoke to her staring at me. A success it was! Luna reminded me of thinking outside the box, to trudge around for unseen solutions!

I learned that Luna could not contain herself off-leash, because there were way too many temptations lurking outside and inside her mind. When she had her mind set, it was ready, set, go—full steam ahead—which was not always in her best interest. One time at my parents' house, something caught her eye and was in her line of sight. Off she went into the road, as a small blue Toyota truck was making its way down the road. Luckily, they were not going too fast, and the truck and Luna both stopped dead in their tracks, and I was able to bring Luna to safety. So, after this, it was leash-on for her safety and my peace of mind. Luna reminded me that sometimes we all have limitations, and it is about embracing them and using them to suit our needs. Luna also reminded me to not take life and ourselves too seriously. A prime example of this is when Luna was doing one of her favorite things—clean-up duty, inspecting, and making sure all spots on the floor were sparkling clean. Well, one day the floor got the best of her. There she stood happily licking the floor away, when, boom, she jumped up with all four paws up, as though she had springs in her paws. Of course, I checked to see what made her go pop pop, but nothing was to be seen. It must have been a bug that scurried away, quickly interrupting her licking. She reminded me in this to not let things always be so serious, to just be in the moment and keep going, and she did not let that stop her from lick-licking away!

Luna loved Christmas! There were many reasons she loved it so. The presents, new toys, special treats were some of her favorite things about this time of year. The absolute best thing for her was that it was the time of year snow came. Luna loved everything about the snow when it was fresh and soft, and she was able to maneuver through it, plowing away. Plow away she did in the snow, skidding her paws through the snow so it would be simply perfect to roll about in. She loved the feel of it on her back and all her paws. She loved the beauty that was the snow and the pure blue wondrous sky. Trampling, walking, and running through the snow also brought her much joy. She was delighted when the snow was still there the next day. She reminded me that it is a must to soak in the opportunity of the snow while it is there, for it was a treasure that only comes at this time of the year.

*Luna enjoying soaking up the snow in her yard
at my parents in Applegate, Oregon*

Chapter Seven

FINDING STRENGTH

After living in Seattle for five years, I found myself once again contemplating a move back to my parents' home. I had two part-time jobs that I enjoyed—one was delivering trays for patients at a hospital, and the other one was as a veterinary assistant/receptionist at a holistic veterinary hospital—but financially I was stressed. I'd also been feeling a little lost in Seattle, and I knew the time had come to leave.

When I moved to Seattle, I gathered more love for myself and embraced all I have to offer, not only for myself, but for my work with animals and their people. I finally got the courage to put myself out there more with my animal communication work and really started to own it and embrace all of it. This all happened by launching my website, getting business cards, and teaching my first-ever animal communication class. It was there that I also did my first radio interview about animal communication. I even co-hosted a weekly radio show. When my spot on that show ended, other things in my life in Seattle had started to crumble. There was a lack of money, even with working two part-time jobs, and my rent was increasing dramatically. Luna helped me to realize that all was not lost—a lot was gained from all of these things—and that sometimes old things give way to make room for new awesomeness in our lives.

I practiced gratitude for my time there, realizing it was just one part of my journey. My sense of worthiness, self-love, and confidence had grown so much, and I was worried I would revert back to the "old" Shawna when I returned to my parents' house. Luna helped me with processing this, and I realized that there was no going back to the old Shawna unless I chose to.

As it turns out, this would be a time of physical healing for me. For years I had suffered from endometriosis. I had undergone one round of surgery years before, but it flared up again, and now I was in pain almost every day. In going back to my parents' home, I had the time and the space to have a hysterectomy. This was one of the best decisions of my life, as I had not realized how much the pain was affecting me. Throughout my recovery, Luna was by my side. She ingrained in me that I'm stronger than I think and know. During this time, if I had a hard day at work, she had a way of knowing and snapping me out of that funk and lifting my spirits. Even if it was a challenge I was facing or just that everyday things were getting me down, Luna helped me find the strength I needed. Luna always knew how my day went.

I remember one rough day when I was still living with my parents. I came home, and my mom just knew something was up because Luna had seemed restless and concerned that day. My dad also saw the communication between Luna and me and could see her old-soul-ness and the connection between Luna and me that ran deep.

After recovery, I continued to do my animal communication work and got my first level of training as a small animal massage therapist with the Northwest School of Animal Massage. Luna was a willing participant in my studies. As I was learning anatomy, I would scope out different areas for practice on Luna to help fine-tune my understanding of the canine body. This skill came in handy as Luna got older because she would get muscle spasms in her hips. Doing some massage on them and energy work helped to ease those spasms. I even got back into radio during this time, hosting my own internet radio show called *Inner Wisdom*. Luna helped me during the show and would often offer up tokens of wisdom for my listeners.

It was time to move and Luna lent a helping hand in the best of ways. As with any move, one tries their best to be organized. Try being the operative word. This one move, I could not seem to find my Sharpie pen. We all know how important these are in a move to determine what is in each box. Then, all of a sudden, my shift focused on Luna, and the location of my Sharpie came to me. This reminded me of how the animals in our life are always eager to help us.

This move was a move of purging for me. As it turns out, I did not have room to get the rest of what I had packed in my car after the U-Haul trailer and truck were packed. You see, I tend to be a bit of a procrastinator. Had I had all my things ready, I might not have been scrambling to figure out where everything was going to fit in my car, including Luna and her two cats, Linnus and Leo. I felt like I was playing a game of Jenga, trying to figure out how everything was going to fit. Mind you, I had already gotten rid of a lot of things for this move to start fresh. How could I still have so much left? It's a good thing there was a Goodwill drop-off location close by for me to take some items that I could replace later. Luna even helped out with purging for this move. I did not have enough room for her crate, so that got donated too, because having room for Luna, Leo and Linnus was more important. As I reflect on it now, it was a good reminder to remember what is important. Finally, everything fit in my car, although it was quite the tight fit. It's a good thing Luna was a trooper as there was not much room for her. She was just happy she had things to brace her on this long drive, as it often seemed Luna wished there was a dog "oh-shit" handle in my car for her to brace herself if I stopped too quickly. Luna was always willing to accommodate me, as I was her. Even though I could hear her thinking, "Oh Shawna, really, this is the most amount of room you can give me," she settled in for the long drive, grateful for stretch breaks and for when we finally arrived at our destination. We were all so happy when we arrived at my parents', as that meant it was time to get out of the car and oh what a relief that was, as we had been on the road for about eight hours. It seemed much longer than that as the exhaustion from the move was kicking in.

At last, a nice bed to crawl into came to me. Luna made herself at home, rolling all about on the bed. During the last few days at our previous apartment, we were sleeping on the couch cushions on the floor. Part of my purging for this move was getting rid of my bed. Luna was not all that thrilled about it, as she liked the comfort of lying on the bed. Lying on the couch cushions did not leave room for both of us, although at first, she thought it did. As I finally made my way to bed for the night, there was Luna on the cushions, leaving nowhere for me to lay. She was not budging. I tried to lie down, but she was insistent on her own comfort. I gave up for a few minutes and thought to myself, "Why not capture this moment?" So, I grabbed my phone to snap a photo. Luna was quite proud of herself, as she was not a fan of dog beds. Why would she need a dog bed when she could share my bed with me, and that was much more comfortable to her. After a few minutes passed, Luna knew how tired I was, so she decided to compromise and let me enjoy the comfort of sleep and the cushions.

This move was to one of Luna's favorite places—back to my parents' house. Luna loved all the sights and smells there and all the adventures to be had. It was back to those ten acres out in the country where all kinds of animals lurked about, and the creek on their property which Luna really enjoyed. Luna offered a lot of support to me during this move, as the cost of living where I was had gotten the best of me, and I was not in the best financial situation.

This was not the easiest move for me. I was moving from a place I had always dreamed of living and leaving a job I loved working as a veterinary receptionist/assistant at a holistic veterinary clinic. I needed time to regroup and get back on track financially. Staying with my parents was the perfect place to do this. Luna reminded me of all the fun there was to be had there and how nice it would be to spend time with my parents. It would give me a chance to be out of the financial stress I was in and help me move forward in my life. She always had a way of showing me and helping me realize new possibilities, even if they were not ones I desired, or thought were possible. Being with her helped ease my mind and allowed me to come up with easeful solutions to help transform my life and create more ease and less financial stress. I was so grateful that she was there to help me navigate during times of transitions, financial stress, and instability.

Being in the nature that surrounded us also helped me, and Luna and I had many grand adventures there. One of them was the great rooster chase. I was at work, and Luna loved spending time outside because there were so many wonderful smells and sights. The front yard was fenced in, and there was a garden that was fenced in as well, which was attached to the front yard. My mom had been working in the garden, and of course, Luna wanted to lend a helping hand. Mom had forgotten that the gate leading out to the barn and chicken coop was not shut. All of a sudden, their rooster came into the garden, strutting about, and it was game on! Luna was out at the starting gate and down for the chase. So, that meant my mom had to get on her feet quickly to avoid the possible catastrophe of a showdown between Luna and the rooster. Luckily, the barn has two small side barns that have doors on the front and rear of them. Thankfully, Luna went into the side barn where the rear door happened to be shut. Mom quickly thought to shut the front door, and she was able to get a hold of Luna to bring her back to safety in the garden, closing the gate behind her. I remember coming home that evening and could feel something interesting had happened that day. I remember looking at Luna; she had a look on her face as if she had something to share with me. I asked my mom if anything had happened that day. She said, "Well, I was not going to tell you," then she proceeded to tell me about the escapade with the rooster. She knew how much I loved Luna and did not want me to be upset. I looked at Luna, and she showed me the humor in the situation, and reminded me that she was safe. This was a reminder that there is always humor to be found even in the stickiest of situations.

That was not the first time Luna had a wild animal encounter that my mom helped with. I guess you never know where adventure will find you. She tried to find a way to make an escape of exploration. It has always been hard for me to find time to relax and to realize just how important taking time to unwind truly is. How it can replenish your heart, soul, and mind—being in a clear space, in the moment, not fretting about any of life's worries. When I was out in nature with Luna, she helped me to find this. Be it a walk outside, a trip to the dog park, or just sitting outside enjoying the moment that lies right before you. Luna and I enjoyed many walks on my parents' property, as well as times discovering and exploring new places. These journeys with her instilled more time to be present in the moment. Before Luna, I thought there were times that I was relaxed, even though I had my phone with me or other things on my mind. Luna helped me to eliminate those distractions and truly take time to be present. Luna also had a slight obsession with firewood, loving to lick it and get all the tasty dirt off it. Well, sometimes, my dad would get in the way of this while he was stacking firewood or starting a fire. Luna had a way of making her disapproval known by nudging him in the butt, and oh boy, did that have a way of getting his attention! That was a lesson in patience for Luna.

Another thing Luna loved doing was insisting her presence be known by lying just outside the kitchen. This always seemed to happen after my dad had left the kitchen, either with some nice, piping hot coffee or hot soup with a sandwich. She would lay right outside the kitchen, all sprawled out, creating a game of Twister for anyone who wanted to pass by Luna to cross into the next room. This was a big bone of contention between her and my dad. Luna always tried to make up for this by giving my dad a kiss on the hand every time she caught him sitting down where one of his hands was in reach.

Around midnight one night, Luna let me know that she needed to go outside and potty. So, I did the usual routine of turning on the porch light and waiting about a minute before opening the door, so any animals that might be outside would have a chance to scurry away, and also to not let any bats in. Luna really had to go, as she was back on the porch very quickly and immensely proud of herself. As she trotted up the stairs, I noticed something in her mouth. I came to realize it was a young opossum. In a quick second, I said, "Luna, drop it," and luckily, she quickly complied. I let her back inside, and thankfully, she and the opossum were both unscathed, as it could have turned out a lot worse. So, here I stood, as I looked at the opossum playing dead on the porch. Thoughts raced through my mind of what to do—I could not just leave the opossum there. So quickly, I found a shovel and somehow managed to coax the opossum onto it. It must have been a sight for Luna to see through the window. Now what to do with this opossum? I did not want to let it stay in the front fenced yard where it and Luna could have a not-so-friendly encounter. So, I opened up the front gate, let the opossum climb off the shovel and under a bush, and hurried quickly back into the front yard, because there were many wild animals that sometimes roamed through my parents' property. I remember coming back into the yard and seeing eyes just staring at me. My first thought was that it was a cougar and that I'd better be quick, then I realized it was just one of the deer that frequented the property.

Luna had many fun rituals that she loved to partake in. The thing is, it was more that Luna and I enjoyed them—my mom and dad did not enjoy them so much. Every morning after we awoke, it was time for Luna to go out and do her morning business. After that was her most favorite part of waking up, her morning bowl of breakfast. Steadfast, she would run into the house and start to tap dance a happy dance for her breakfast. The thing was, my parents had hardwood floors and, well, when Luna would tap, she tapped all about on the hardwood floor. Let me just say that Luna left a little piece of herself there. What she reminded me about in these morning tap routines was to remember to find joy in the simplest of things, and be grateful for every day you have.

Luna and I also had many of our own rituals. I have a bit of a sweet tooth. Luna must have been curious about what that was all about and wanted to partake in this pleasure with me. One of my favorite cookies is E.L. Fudge cookies. Well, one day, I decided to break the cookie up into two pieces, the one with the fudge and cookie and the side with just the cookie. Luna must have thought that I was breaking the two pieces apart for her, and from that moment on, every time I had an E.L. Fudge, I had to break it in half and share the non-chocolate side with Luna. If I did not, she let me know that it is important to share with those you love, even if it means sharing one of your most favorite treats.

 She even tried to share one of her favorite treats with me, and let me just say it was not something I was eager to have or wanted to share with her. It was one treat I would let her enjoy on her own. You are probably wondering what this treat could possibly have been. Well, Luna and I shared our life with two cats, Leo and Linnus. Luna loved what I like to call "Kitty Roca," and for those of you that have cats, I am sure you are familiar with what Kitty Roca is. For those who are not familiar, it is quite the delectable treat for dogs that comes straight out of the litterbox. I am sure you have figured out by now what I am referring to. Luna thought she was just being helpful, and the bonus was she got to partake in a tasty, scrumptious treat. Well, one day, she gave me a reminder of how she helped keep the litterbox clean. I came home to find the litter scoop flipped up at the opening of the litterbox, the scoop toward the opening and the handle sat perfectly on the floor. This could only have been a reminder from Luna about how much she helped maintain the litterbox. Or perhaps she and the cats were in cahoots, telling me that I needed to keep up the same pace with cleaning it as Luna did. Whatever it was, it was definitely a reminder to me that my animals, whether I realized it or not, were always sending me gentle nudges of communication.

Luna also reminded me to live without inhibitions and just go for it. One day, as she reminded me of this, I got the message loud and clear. We were at one of her favorite places, the dog park near where we lived, and Luna decided to cut loose in the grass, rolling all about. She was having a grand old time! Then, she got up and her back was brown. I exclaimed to myself, "Was it muddy there?" Well, that thought left my mind the closer Luna got to me—the smell was undeniable. There were a lot of different water areas at this particular dog park, but that surely was not an option, because I did not want to make poopy water—that would have been gross. Thankfully, I remembered they happened to have a dog washing station, so off we went to get her all cleaned up. She was not as upset as I was, as she had fun and was focused on the fun she had just experienced. Finally, we reached the dog wash station, but I had no cash with me, and cash is what they needed. Luckily, they could see my dilemma and let me wash off Luna. Thank goodness for their generosity; otherwise, the car ride home would have been, well, less than enjoyable.

That experience made me even more thankful for the things that Luna rolled in that were much more pleasant. Luna loved the snow—especially the fresh snow that she could burrow and roll around in. She would roll and roll in it, then she would make a dive bomb into the snow, sliding her front feet, making the perfect place to burrow in it. Then she would flip on her back, rolling all about in the snow. Then, when that spot was all "rolled out," she would find a fresh spot to roll all about in. This was a reminder to have fun and keep the path open for new adventures, always finding your own way. I treasured the times in the snow with Luna. To see and feel the happiness it brought her made my heart gleam with joy.

A reminder to have fun came with the snow during one of those experiences with Luna. We were out walking in the snow; it was deep, and, well, my feet got ahead of me. I found myself falling and I landed in the snow. I gazed at Luna, remembering how important laughter is, and laughter burst out of me. Luna and I made angels in the snow. It was as though she was so happy that I was partaking in this with her. She must have wondered what took me so long to enjoy this fun with her.

One fall I had with Luna was not so fun. We were out on our morning walk. The grass happened to be extra muddy that day due to the sprinklers that run at night and to a fresh rain. It was taking Luna an extra-long time to do her morning business. We were walking all about, and I could feel my frustration rise as I had to get going to work. Well, let's just say that did not work out too well for me. Luna pulled me in a different direction, and we happened to be on a little bit of a slope, when suddenly, I lost my footing, and down into the mucky, muddy, wet grass I went. It must have somehow released tension, making me more relaxed, and in turn, making Luna more relaxed. Almost directly after that, Luna finished her business. I was so happy to get back inside and so grateful I had not showered yet, as that was exactly what was in order after this ordeal.

This whole escapade changed my mindset for times when I happened to be running late. I came to the realization that Luna had picked up on the rush I was in and, well, let's just say we canceled each other out. Meaning that this rushed energy I was putting out was like an amplifier magnifying all I was feeling. Luna wanted to please me and had picked up on this, but did the opposite of what I actually wanted her to do. Hmm, that was an interesting revelation—the more I focused on being calm, the calmer Luna would become. Could it be that simple? Well, indeed, it was that simple. When I shifted this focus on our walks, it made a huge positive impact for both Luna and me. From this moment on, whenever I felt rushed, Luna reminded me of this lesson. How amazing it was to have such reflection from my girl.

Of course, I wanted to make sure to keep her entertained and content because of all the happiness and joy she brought to my world and to me every day. I would sometimes leave the TV on for her to enjoy, just so she had some background noise and something to keep her company. She always seemed to enjoy the company of the TV—well, most of the time, that is. There was one show that she did not seem to particularly enjoy. Every time it was on, she had a look of annoyance on her face. I happened to really enjoy the humor in this show, so I wondered why and how she did not enjoy *I Love Lucy*, but she did not enjoy it at all. The response that came to me from her was, "Just because you find it funny doesn't mean I find it entertaining." We all have our own sense of humor and, well, that was just not her kind of humor, because she did not really care for Lucille Ball or the sound of her voice. I was astonished—how could she dislike, not only the show *I Love Lucy*, but Lucille Ball as well? I was blown away, to say the very least. She reminded me in that moment, that we all have our own ideas of what we find humorous, and just because something is funny now, does not mean it will always be funny to us. Just because something is supposed to be a certain way does not mean that is how it is supposed to be for everyone. Find humor where humor exists for you. Who knows who else you will enlighten or find has the humor you do? If not, at least you have the humor that is for you. Too many times, we choose to follow along with others' definitions of things instead of going with our own definition of what is for us. Although it was not Luna's favorite, she enjoyed it from time to time, which reminded me there were more important things, like getting exercise and spending time outside. Getting out helps us be in our own energy—do not get me wrong—sometimes being in the moment of just watching TV is okay from time to time.

Having all of our focus on one thing is not always a good thing. Well, according to Luna, unless that one thing was taking her for a walk. She taught me the importance of focusing on the walk and not my phone, and to not bring my phone with me or leave it in my back pocket and only remove it if there was a picture to be taken or if I had a thought to jot down. This was a good reminder to stay focused and not miss anything on the walk, and to enjoy the moment with my Luna. This also reminded me of how many times I had missed out on the moment in front of me by having my mind cluttered with things that distracted me from the very moment that was right in front of me to enjoy.

One morning, Luna and I went for a nice walk before work. We had just made her morning deposit into the trash, and we were headed back home so I could get ready for work that afternoon. We walked upon the grass, taking a shortcut and for a change of scenery. The grass was still wet from its morning watering and was slightly uneven and sloped downward. As I was walking along, I suddenly lost my footing in a muddy, wet spot and went down on my rear. After I fell, I remember looking at Luna, who just stood right by my side. I was quite frustrated with myself. I remember turning to Luna and what came to me from her was that sometimes we lose our balance, and we need not let that get us down. That there will always be a way for us to get back up again. We must not let small annoyances get in our way. That instead, we must pick ourselves back up again and see the humor in the moment after the frustration. I remember as soon as I soaked this in, Luna looked at me with a glow and a wink, as if saying, "You got it, my Shawna." Our relationship was one of unconditional mutual support.

Luna loved mealtimes, and not just *her* mealtimes. She thought all the mealtimes, even those that were not hers, were hers. When we were staying with my parents, she loved the opportunity of having extra meals; she loved to watch anyone who happened to be eating. She did not like it when my mom would give her the "pillow block"—as in, Mom would block what she was eating with a pillow, Luna was not happy when she lost sight of how much was left to eat because she could only see how many bites were being taken. Her frustration with this would not stop her persistent gaze at the food bounty she wanted all for herself. She stood firm in her stance and stared, hoping that one of my parents would be kind enough to share even the tiniest of bites with her. She always knew she could count on her Shawna to share. She reminded me in this to hold fast to your desires and always treasure the bounty that awaits you.

Luna always had a way of getting me out of a funk. There was a funk I especially needed help getting out of while I was living on my parents' beautiful piece of property. It was always fun to explore with Luna to see what kind of nature we might come across. Even with all this beauty, something was lacking in my life, and I found myself to be bored and unfulfilled. The nearest town was about 30 minutes away, which seemed like an eternity to get to, and to be completely honest, there was not much there that tickled my fancy. I truly enjoyed the quiet time being at my parents' with Luna. I also enjoyed having the time to spend with my parents as I had been so accustomed to living alone. It was always nice to have their company, don't get me wrong, but I still very much enjoyed my alone time. It was about finding a balance between alone time and time with my parents, which was not always easy for me to balance. Good thing for my Luna, as she helped me to balance out that time.

I had been living at my parents' for almost two years and had an itch to move into my own place again, with more room to have my own space, other than just my bedroom. I had such a longing for that, yet I was worried about going out on my own again. Would I be able to do it? Did I have enough money saved up? Was I truly ready to be on my own again? As I would tune into Luna, I could feel an insistence coming from her, as if she were saying, "Oh, Shawna, what are you going to do for yourself?" I was not really happy, as living in Southern Oregon was not my type of climate, and I felt lost down there. I had often thought about going back to the Portland, Oregon and Vancouver, Washington area again. Was this what I really wanted? Would things crumble there as they did in Seattle? Would the people I knew there embrace the new Shawna? I had grown so much and was not the unsure, insecure, unconfident girl I was when I left there. The many years with Luna had helped me be full of certainty, secureness in all I was, and 100% confident in who I was.

With Luna's help and her sure steadfast, determined nature, I was able to muster up the courage to start checking out my options, knowing full well that I could still keep to who I had become without slipping back into old patterns. What a gift this was that Luna helped me to discover! The search was on, and I started applying for jobs and scoping out potential places to live. Then, after a successful round of interviews, the time came for a working interview as a Doctor's Assistant at an emergency animal hospital. What a perfect fit and opportunity I had before me! The working interview went great, and about a week later, I got the call offering me the position. Doubts started to cross through my mind—would I be able to find a place to live in a timely matter? Would I be able to afford this new place? Whenever these thoughts crossed my mind, I would look into Luna's eyes or spend some time with her outside, sitting on the porch or walking my parents' property. This was just what I needed to get me out of my own way.

Finally, the perfect place came up, which happened to be at an apartment complex I had already looked at when I had been in the area for my working interview. It was about ten minutes from my new job. As luck would have it, one unit had just come open. It was a good thing that I had been guided to take an application home with me when I first looked at that property. I scrambled to get it all filled out before someone else turned in an application for the same unit. Luna reminded me to simmer down and relax, as I scrambled about. It was as though she was reassuring me that it would all work out. And work out it did! I got my application in and paid the application fee over the phone. Whew, what a relief that was. That was, until I found out I had to make a trip up there to sign paperwork in person before the moving-in process was going to happen. I wondered how on earth I would have the time to make a trip up there for this? Then, once again, my focus shifted to Luna, and my mind eased. I decided to bring her with me for the four-and-a-half-hour car ride, and she was a great travel companion. It was a quick, flawless trip. Excitement set in, as it was now time for our next grand adventure, which happened to be way more significant than I first realized—a time for Luna and me to be in our own space together. Time to be treasured, as it was about eight months after that move that I got Luna's cancer diagnosis.

*Luna running up from the front yard at my parents' house
in Applegate, Oregon*

Chapter Eight

INNER WISDOM

Luna taught me to listen within and listen to myself. I had always looked to others to validate me and would often go with their insights instead of following my own guidance. Luna helped me to start listening to my own guidance. I listened for guidance for me and for her as well. I remember one time when I intuitively knew to get a second opinion from another vet. Luna was losing a lot of fur, and this was way more than the normal shedding she had. I knew there was something more going on. This comes up often in my sessions with my clients. Our pets do not have a voice in the veterinarian's office. We are their advocates. Trusting our inner guidance and getting a second opinion when needed regarding an issue that has not been able to be resolved is a topic that I have had many examples of from my clients. On the other side of this, Luna reminded me to remember that I was more supported than I realized, as I have not always been good at asking for help, thinking I could do it all on my own. Luna reminded me that it is okay to ask for help and that there is always support available when I need it. And that it is not a sign of weakness to ask for help, it can actually be a sign of strength.

There was a painful time during our first two years together when I had thoughts about rehoming Luna. I was working so much and struggling to make ends meet, and the doubts of others rang loud in my head. I even found a person for Luna to go meet. But my heart did not feel right about it. How could I not have Luna be a part of my everyday life? She meant so much to me, and I knew she was happy with me by the way she looked in my eyes. I listened to my inner wisdom and realized that what I had was more than enough for Luna. I ended up realizing she wanted to be there for me regardless of what others' thoughts were or how much time or money I had, that what I had was enough for Luna. We were together to look out for and care for each other. I knew I could not bear to give Luna up, nor could she bear not having me in her life.

As mentioned earlier, at one point in Luna's life she started losing extra fur. Not just the normal amount of shedding that any dog has, especially Labs. Luna would leave what I would call Luna tumbleweeds of fur all about the floor. Well, at this point in her life, it happened to be a significant amount more fur than usual. Concerned about this, I reached out to Luna's primary veterinarian. They didn't seem to find this to be unusual. Something in my gut knew it was more than only normal shedding. I made an appointment with a local holistic veterinarian, and I went over all my concerns about this and how Luna had shown some early signs of Cushing's disease from some prior bloodwork. This vet checked her over using Chinese medicine principles. This appointment looked at all that was going on with her. It was nice to have all my concerns addressed and be heard.

I ended up making some changes after this appointment. I started Luna on some Chinese herbs, another supplement, and incorporated some raw meat and veggies into Luna's diet. Not being a big meat eater, I was not thrilled about prepping the raw meat, but if it would help my girl, I was all for it. The vet recommended a local butcher shop to get a five-pound log of a four-meat mixture for her. It came time to make the meat patties, and someone was thrilled about it, but it sure was not me. Luna loved watching me prepare the patties for her. The only thing she did not like was to have to wait for them to be all ready to go, as if she had been waiting for hours for me to finish her patties. Of course, after I was done, I gave in to her "Give me some—this is torture," look. Luna was so happy to have this delectableness as a part of her daily diet. She even liked how veggies were mixed with her patty, dry food, and warm water. She would give me a look of despair when I was out of her patties. Giving them to her with the other things solved the extra shedding that had been going on with her. This was an important reminder that I knew when something was off with my Luna and to trust that knowingness. For I not only owed that to myself to trust my intuition, but I also owed it to my girl.

This was also a reminder to be gentle with the other vet as they were just going by their own beliefs and knowledge. The thing was, I had to follow mine. Luna would also watch as I chopped up organic carrots. I would occasionally toss her one of the carrot pieces. She enjoyed it but would have much rather have had a piece of a meat patty. She would have also much preferred the carrots be already chopped—not to save me the work in chopping—but, because she favored the precut crinkle carrot for their size and perfect textured crunch, and it was way easier on her teeth. So, once I made this discovery, it was the crinkle carrots she got. She did love other veggies as a snack, such as broccoli, cauliflower, cabbage, green beans, and of course, carrots. The one veggie she did not like at all was lettuce. I remember trying to give her a piece. I held it up to her, thinking, of course, she would grab it right away, and I better be mindful of my fingers. Well, this is one time I did not need to be mindful of that, which was quite out of the norm. Instead of grabbing the lettuce, she curled up her lips and turned her face away. There was no way of talking her into it—she must have thought it was a disgusting green slimy thing. So, I knew I dared not offer her that again. This was a good reminder that just because something is offered to you does not mean you have to take it. Especially if it is something you do not like to eat. It is as important to be polite to ourselves as it is to be polite to others. This goes not only for food, but also for putting our happiness at the forefront of who we are and doing what makes our heart flutter with happiness, for we all deserve that kind of happiness. It is about having happiness in the simplest of things.

Luna was always pleased with the simple pleasures of joy that came her way and enjoyed every moment of them. One of her favorite games was what I like to call the fir cone game. See, Luna taught me that what is normal for one is not necessarily that way for all. Most labs enjoy a good game of fetch with a tennis ball. Well, Luna liked tennis balls; however, fetching with them was not her favorite. Her favorite fetch game was with fir cones. My parents had quite the supply of fir cones in their yard. You could say it was a smorgasbord of fir cones for Luna—so many to choose from. She would grab one and run around the yard with it, occasionally dropping it for me to throw for her. Then the chase was on. It was as though she was fascinated with all the different shapes and sizes of them. When she was done with the fir cones, sometimes, she would switch to a nice stick that she would run around the yard with. She loved to go round and round in circles, which was proof that sometimes going round and round in circles helps us clarify exactly what we need. Luna would remind me of this when she would stop for a second and then go in another direction—a reminder that a shift in focus can really be that simple. A simple turn in direction with a quick step is sometimes exactly what we need.

One day while walking near my parents' home, Luna took that advice quite literally. We were walking back to the house, getting ready to head back inside, and, well, let's just say my car was in the way and delayed our trip back inside. As we were walking by my car, it was as if the passenger side mirror jumped out at Luna. Suddenly, Luna jumped towards me. She made a small jolt, and bam, in a quick second, she ran into the mirror with the side of her face. She did not stop after that quick jump towards me; she just kept on going as if nothing had happened. Luna took pride in remaining graceful in inopportune moments. I was more stunned by the experience than Luna was, as I remember being in such dismay from this and worried that my girl was hurt. She conveyed to me, "I am okay, my Shawna; it was just a little bump in the road, and let's keep moving on with our walk." This still sticks with me to this day because it really struck a chord of how profound this one experience was, and how many other experiences of small bumps in the road that I had experienced in my life. Had I kept going, moving on, or did I use these experiences as a crutch to catapult me back into the resistance I held onto from those experiences? What a reflection this was for me of the times I had held myself back from greatness by allowing a little bump in the road to hold me back. What a shining example of how even the smallest bit of perseverance is important to remember, for the small steps can lead to even bigger steps. Luna was such a great fountain of reflection, knowledge, and wisdom for me.

Linnus developed a lump on his leg, and he was not moving around much, was very warm, and not eating much, so I set up an appointment with the vet. They did a needle aspirate of the lump on his leg where they inserted a needle into the lump to see if it had any cancer cells. It turned out to be cancer. Linnus was declining very rapidly. He was not himself—he would barely move, was not wanting to eat, his body temperature was warm, and he had a distinctive smell coming from his body from the cancer. It all happened so fast between noticing the lump and his fast decline. It was on a Saturday that the cancer was revealed, and two days later, Monday, when a hard decision was in the air. I had to make some decisions that were his wishes, not what I wanted, but what he wanted. I happened to be at work that day and Linnus had been on my mind the entire morning. At this time, we were living with my parents, so I called to check in on him during my break, and my mom let me know he was not doing well at all. How was I to make this decision and know it was the right one to make for him? I knew the decision I had to make was not easy. It was not about me; it was about Linnus and what was best for him. I had a piece of paper in front of me and wrote yes on one side and no on the other side of the paper to help me process this hard decision that was upon me. I tuned into Linnus and asked what was best for him, with the question, "Is it time?" to Linnus in my mind. He had me close my eyes to not sway my choice. I used a pen to guide me. It was guided to yes, that it was time to say goodbye, which I knew, but just needed some extra confirmation.

On my lunch break, I was able to get an appointment for that afternoon. I left work early and had never felt such a rush to get home, as I did not have much time before his appointment and I wanted to spend some time with Linnus, as this all had come on so fast. I only had about 20 minutes before it would be time to head off to the vet. It happened on Winter Solstice, which was fitting, as Linnus had a very grounded presence. It was very fitting that he chose this day to make his transition. It was especially important for Leo and Luna to say their goodbyes to Linnus, so I wanted to make sure Luna and Leo had a chance to say their goodbyes. Leo did not want anything to do with Linnus. It was as if he knew about what was going on and it was hard for him. Luna gave him a sniff sealed with love.

We arrived at the vet, and the receptionist who checked us in had had a similar experience with her dog. The universe always provides us with support. There was the cutest dog in the lobby. Normally if I see any dog, I would naturally want to pet them. This time I had a pull not to. It was for my Linnus that I felt this pull, as he wanted the comfort of Luna and Leo with him and their scent and energy. In petting another dog, that energy chain would not be the same. Keeping that energy the same was important, not only for Linnus, but it was also important for Luna and Leo, as they were my trio. Linnus passed very peacefully. I was able to provide him comfort and love. I wanted to have some of Linnus's fur, so the vet cut off some of his fur and put it in a little zipped plastic bag. Then it was time to take him home to bury him.

We arrived back home, and I felt the urge to bury Linnus right away. It was as though his body wanted to be back with the earth. I wanted to show Linnus's body to Luna and Leo. Leo clearly let me know he did not want to see Linnus, as it would have been too much for him. So, I honored that. Luna, on the other hand, wanted to give Linnus a quick sniff to pay her respects. My dad helped me prepare Linnus's grave in their front yard. Luna sat and watched the whole time, overseeing the process. As I knew it was important for her to be a part of it and to offer support to me.

The time came to put Linnus to rest. I put Linnus in his resting place and stood back a moment to catch my breath. Then, at that moment, Luna went and sat right down on top of his grave to pay her respects. I was so touched and moved by this whole experience. It was as though she was one with his presence. I really wanted to capture this moment, so I quickly ran back inside to grab my phone. Just as I came out with my phone, Luna walked away from where she had been sitting. *How could I not have captured this moment?* I thought to myself.

My focus shifted to Luna, and she reminded me sometimes it is the moments we capture with our hearts and mind's eye that are to be saved in our memories and in our heart. Because that is where we can capture the memory in its purest form, where it brings our mind and focus to that memory and sparks the connection that lies inside the memory. The memories captured with our hearts can be the most profound of them all.

Linnus always used to lay by the left side near the second pillow on my bed. The night he passed, I really missed his presence. I remember laying in my bed, being drawn to put my left hand on the pillow to the left of me. All of a sudden, through the pillow, I could feel Linnus's presence. I felt his paw in my hand and could feel the heartbeat of his paw in my hand. I enjoyed being in this moment as it brought me much comfort. He wanted to remind me that the heartbeat of his presence will always be there within me. He also reminded me that all I had to do was ask, and that is all it took for his presence to beckon itself to me. This was a reminder to notice the signs we may otherwise dismiss. When we give space for these signs, they show up. It is when we question them that draws them away from us.

Linnus sent me many signs. The day after his passing, I felt the urge to flip through the Sirius radio stations in my car. It pulled me to a song I had never heard before, and I felt compelled to keep listening as it spoke to me. I tuned into the song, the words were as follows, "Do not let the sun catch you crying." I knew this was Linnus sending me a song to brighten my day. This was confirmed even more after this song, as I was pulled to another channel. A Bon Jovi Christmas song came on and the words, "Bells will be ringing," spoke to me for many reasons. I loved Bon Jovi, and the words were another message from my boy. The part about the bells was significant, as it was a reminder that he was always just a ring away.

I remember looking at pictures of Linnus, Leo, and Luna after his passing. In one picture, a ball of light appeared, sparkled, and then went away—a sign that Linnus's presence and energy were still very much a part of us. This would be the first Christmas without my sweet Linnus Magnus Pie, which just happened to be the nickname he chose for himself. It was hard knowing his physical presence would not be with us on Christmas. I awoke that Christmas morning to find the light in my bedroom was on. I was perplexed at first then it all made sense. It was Linnus sending his light and love over us on Christmas morning, which warmed my heart and put a smile of joy on my day.

There was another night after his passing when I had heard a hairball coughing sound that was not Leo's hairball coughing sound. All cats have their own unique sounds, and that was in no way Leo's. I knew that was Linnus, watching over us. I remember the next day at work, I felt my hair move like someone was combing through it— a sign from Linnus that he was there to help get me through the day. I had felt bad about not knowing about his cancer sooner. The message that came through from him about this was as follows, "Sometimes it's okay to tune things out, as we might not supposed to be tuning into them at that moment." This message from him really spoke to me and helped me realize his thoughts on all of this. I had honored his wishes and that was what he wanted me to remember. This was a reminder that sometimes we get caught up in our human emotions and lose focus on the animals in our lives. He reminded me of the importance of factoring in all outcomes and possibilities when faced with a situation like this, and that it's not about beating ourselves up about what should have, could have, or would have, but instead focusing on the moment.

Luna always was inspiring to me to be a better listener. She was not fond of loud noises that pierced her ears and pulsated through her whole body. One time during our stay at my parents' place comes to mind in particular. It was a beautiful day with a bright, clear, blue sky—a perfect day for Luna to enjoy fresh air, and the scents and smells of the pure, fresh, country air. Or so I thought, until I heard gunshots, which was sometimes not so uncommon in the country. I was inside catching up on some things, as it happened to be my day off. I heard the gunshots, but they stopped quickly, so I did not really give it a second thought. Well, that was, until I heard the front door slamming open. That for sure caught my attention, as did the sound of Luna's paws pitter-pattering across the floor. Before I shut the front door, I noticed there were scratches on it where Luna had pawed at it to get in, which for sure had paid off, because she managed to get the door open, which I thought I had closed all the way. Good thing that my Luna was always persistent and never gave up. She reminded me in this moment to keep scratching the surface that will get you to your desires. From that point on, I was better at keeping track of noises outside when Luna was out there. She reminded me in this to always keep focus, as sometimes we are not always paying attention as our minds get busy and we lose sight of what we really need to be paying attention to at that moment. Luna always took great care of me, always having concern for me and my well-being.

One night, I got up at about 2:00 a.m. to let Luna out, and there stood a guy with cold intent in his eyes wearing a black hooded sweatshirt. His stare was focused completely on us, and Luna and I did not like that. Luna gave him a glance, as she knew that was what she needed to do at the moment to not antagonize him. Fortunately, she had just finished her business. After that glance, Luna and I knew it was time to head back inside. There was no dilly-dallying; we did not engage and went calmly and directly inside. I knew Luna always had my back.

Luna had quite the combination of skin and ear issues during her lifetime. A big paw licker she was—she loved to lick and lick at her paws. She also had a spot on her right front leg that was a bone of contention for her and for me, because it would heal, then come back again, and then heal again. I was at my wit's end with this, as I knew it bothered her. Many solutions were tried—there was this spray and that spray—but none of them worked 100%. Many trips to the vet were made regarding this "hot spot" known as a lick granuloma. Part of this was that it had become a habit for her. Finally, I realized the more anxious I was about something going on in my life, the more Luna licked at it. Could it be that a part of this was her trying to help me with my anxiety? I noticed the more I was aware of this affecting her, and used tools to help ease any anxiousness, the more it helped her to refrain from licking at it. It solved part of the issue, not all of it, so in doing some research, I discovered grain-free food. So, why not give it a try, as I had pretty much almost exhausted my other options. It did the trick—the sore finally healed completely and did not come back. Yippee! Luna's vet was amazed by this; it was as if she could not believe her eyes. She was happy that it had healed up. In this instance, Luna reminded me of how in tune we were to each other's energy and emotions, and to listen to the little signs from her of how she wanted to help me by bringing ease into my mind.

At the vet, Luna walked in with a presence as big as a bubble surrounding her. She would glide in full of the utmost, purest, confidence and presence—steadfast, she was. She was beyond that of making her presence be remembered; as she meandered about, she would leave little fragments of her hair on the floor, making little tumbleweeds all over it. You could see the happiness this brought her, as she was so proud to walk from this magnificent splendor of her fur. The most pride came when she noticed the front desk person had seen the tuffs of her wondrous fur that were dancing across the floor. She gazed back with a nod, as if saying, "That is me. A sparkle of me to brighten your day. A distraction from being behind the front desk." Luna loved bestowing moments of wisdom in her encounters with others. She reminded me to leave a little sparkle of yourself wherever you go.

Luna often reminded me of the importance of finding comfort in the most comfortable place you can find—once she found comfort, she went with it. One day I found her in what I did not believe to be an ideal comfortable place. Leo had a basket of toys, and I found Luna with her head rested just so on the edge of his toy basket. She was tired for a nap, so she plopped herself down in the first spot she found. She had no interest in dog beds; she preferred to find a place to lay that was of her own choosing. One night while spending the night at my parents' house, I awoke to find Luna comfortably rested up in the leather recliner that was right next to where I slept. Talk about taking advantage of the perfect spot, as I was sleeping on an air mattress, and Luna wanted nothing to do with those. She did not like the way they moved about because it made her feel like she was on an unsteady ship. Her most favorite place to lay was with Leo on the bed or on the couch. They loved bringing each other comfort. Luna and Leo had many moments of lying together. There is a picture I captured of them when Leo first entered our lives and one towards the end of Luna's life that are almost identical to each other, just showing how important familiar comfort is.

*Luna reflecting looking over Thompson Creek at my parent's
house in Applegate, Oregon*

Chapter Nine

SAYING GOODBYE

One of my favorite adventures with my Luna was a trip to the coast that we took for my birthday. We left about 9:00 a.m. on a cool, bright, sunny day and headed for Cannon Beach, Oregon. We got settled in for the approximate two-hour drive there. It was such a beautiful day, and sometimes, a girl and her dog just need a day of adventure together, soaking in the smells and sights on the coast. We started the day by walking down the beach and soaking up all that the sand and fresh salt air had to offer us. Then it was time to explore a nearby nature trail, which ended up being short-lived, as the beach was beaconing us back to it. Some shallow-water called to Luna to lie in, so there we were led, and there I was reminded by Luna to let yourself be guided to the adventure that awaits you. She plopped herself down in the water, enjoying the calm and peace the water brings to one's soul. Shortly after that, we found a perfect log to sit on to soak the water and sand into and at our feet—bringing center and calm to us both, enjoying this moment of just being present.

Along the way, we captured some pictures, and Luna always reminded me that sometimes it's the memories that capture more than a picture can, for it allows us to focus on the memory and remember things we might not have remembered. The day turned into afternoon, and it soon became lunchtime. So, it was time to see what awaited us for lunch. When one is on the coast, seafood is a treasure to be enjoyed. We went into town, walked about and found this restaurant that had outdoor seating, because why would one want to sit inside when they could be outside enjoying the nice, fresh, salty air? That for sure made the place to stop Bill's Tavern. The atmosphere was friendly and quaint. The ambiance of the same calm as the beach stayed with us there. I ordered the codfish and chips, which was beyond amazing. Luna enjoyed some of my fries, as how could I not share with her.

After lunch, a stroll around town was in order. We found a great pet store, and as we meandered in, they had silver buckets of treats right at Luna's nose. Luna was always very well-mannered—unless there was something she wanted. As I was looking about the store seeing all they had to offer, I was not concerned about what Luna may or may not be doing. Then suddenly, Luna turned her head to me with a chicken foot in her mouth. Little did I know, but Luna was a shoplifter, or should I say paw-grabbing chicken foot stealer? So, of course, I went up and paid for the chicken foot Luna was enjoying. I saw how much she was enjoying this delicacy, so of course, I had to buy her another one, as one cannot just enjoy one chicken foot. This was a reminder to treat yourself to special treats and to enjoy them. Strolling through town, we found another pet store to explore, but to Luna's disappointment, there were no treats at nose level. So, it was time to head back to the beach.

Before we headed down the water, we found a nice bench to sit on and enjoy the sounds and smell of the fresh ocean air. Luna was in heaven, as there was concrete to lay on—she had a love affair with the feel of concrete and the warmth it brought her. It was a day of being in the moment, outside of time and space—just being, not worrying about what time it was or things that needed to get done the next day. Back to the beach we went, enjoying the sound and water at our feet. There was no hurry or expectation about how far we would walk. The sun was starting to fade, so we ended up driving to another nearby coastal town. The energy was more chaotic there, so we decided to head back to Cannon Beach to bring the wonderful calm and peace from the day back. Then, the reason for this side trip came to my awareness. We passed a rock shop that was going out of business, so of course I had to stop, and there I found a beautiful piece of clear quartz that I knew I had to buy. It now lives on a cabinet with some of the rocks and shells Luna and I picked up from the beach. To me, this crystal symbolizes the clear connection we had and still have to this day.

On our way back to Cannon Beach, we saw a beautiful herd of elk to the right of us. This memory reminds me of the strength my Luna gives me still. We did one quick walk down the coast again, then Luna let me know it was time to go, as she was starting to become tired. In order to get back to the car, there was a big set of stairs, about ten, for us to go up, then a turn up to about five more stairs. We made it up the ten stairs, but when it came time to come up the last five stairs, my Luna's back end became weak. I remember standing there thinking, *Now what are we going to do to get back to the car?* I gazed at

Luna and heard her say, "Shawna, we got this. We are always each other's strength, and I will help you help me." She showed me how to support her back end, and up to the top of the stairs we went. We looked at each other with a sense of accomplishment and joy. This was a reminder that the relationship we have with our pets is a partnership. When we were back at the car, Luna looked at me, and I knew that jumping up into the backseat would have been too much for her. I assured her I would help her up, and I could see the relief she felt when she was back in the car. It was about 9:00 p.m., a beautiful evening on the beach, as we headed back home to soundly sleep. Luna always reminded me how amazing it was to have open communication with her and how that made our bond even stronger.

Some realizations came to me that day that I was not ready for—that my Luna was getting older, and we had to treasure each moment together. I understand now that it was hard for me to imagine my life without my girl. That was my last birthday with my Luna, which is why that day is still so important to me, as it is a reminder of her presence that still very much exists, just in a different way. As crazy as it sounds, at times since she has passed, her presence is with me now more than ever. And she sends me signs of that presence. The presence of her hums and sings within my soul and vibrates light and love to every part of me. Of course, I miss her physical presence, but her spiritual presence is very much alive within me. All I have to do is think of her, and a sign shows itself to me, makes its way to me. Or, if I am struggling with something, a message or sign from her comes to me out of the blue.

A reminder to be open to those signs, for when we are open to them and having them come to us, they do. It is something we have to look for as we might miss it. Being open to the possibilities opens a new kind of awareness. Luna often reminded me of this on car rides, and I often think to myself that I wish Luna was here as well to experience it. She reminded me that even though she's not physically with me, she's more physically with me now, as her presence is now limitless.

Fourth of July is not one of my favorite holidays. The one reason for that is due to the fireworks, and the effect fireworks have on animals—both wild and domestic—and people with PTSD, and also the risk of fires. I feel fireworks should be left to the professionals. It was the Fourth of July of 2016, and little did I know this was going to be my last Independence Day with my girl. We awoke in the morning, and Luna was not herself—she was out of sorts. Her body was off-balance, her head was slanted and not straightforward, and there was a slight slant. It was very noticeable, and my Luna had brought it to my attention. You see, you probably have had a similar experience, as our animals have a way of giving us little nudges and bringing attention to things that are going on with them. It may not be something we notice right away; sometimes the thought of it will come to our attention at another time. Luna let me know to relax, breathe, and just keep an eye on her. So, I tuned in to her, confirming that this is what she wanted. Sure, I could have taken her to the vet, but I honed into the intuition of my work with animals, and it came to me she had a vestibular incident, which is common in older dogs. I kept her quiet and comfortable and did some energy work and massage on her.

Then came the time where I needed to take her outside to relieve herself, contemplating what I was going to do, as I lived upstairs, and her back legs were uneasy. *Would she be able to make it make up the stairs?* I wondered to myself. So, here I was downstairs with my Luna at the bottom of the stairs, and I knew she would not be able to make it back up the stairs without some sort of sling. My mind and thoughts were all over the place and filled with panic. Thoughts were racing about how I was going to get back upstairs with my girl.

Suddenly, I heard "Stop" inside my head out of nowhere. So, I focused my attention on Luna, and I could feel her energy guiding me to my car. So, of course, I went to my car, and on my way there, I remembered the sheet that was laid on the back seat. Time to improvise, so I ended up making a makeshift sling with a sheet. Let me tell you, this did not come easy. Out came the sheet, and I put it under Luna's belly by her back legs and brought the two ends up, holding them together to offer her support for her back end and hind legs. I held her leash with the two ends of the sheet. Up the stairs we went—slow and steady with each step. What a relief it was to make it back up. For the next couple of days, I kept Luna inside to give her body a chance to rest and recover. Thank goodness for pee pads; they were my saving grace allowing time for Luna to heal. A couple of days passed, and Luna started to improve.

The true test of this came when it was time to venture outside again. We took it slowly together, with the communication between us remaining open. Before we meandered down the stairs, we looked at each other as though we were at the starting line of a big race. With that look into each other's eyes, we spoke to one another, "We've got this." So, down the stairs we went. We came to the grass, and I saw the spark of happiness in Luna as she looked around, and the joy as she felt the sun in her eyes. Then, she did her outside business. She was so happy to kick her feet back in the grass. Her legs were still a little bit wobbly and off-balance—the best way I know how to describe it is how one walks if they have had a little too much to drink. Then, she plopped herself down in the grass and lay there with a smile in her heart, on her face, and in her eyes. She felt the grass and sun as they soothed her soul. Her wish of being outside again was fully alive as she lay right next to a beautiful dandelion.

With time she recovered. Within a few days, her head was straight forward again, and she started to not have the wobble as she walked. This time brought a lot of reflection about Luna and her age. It brought the realization of the fact that she was getting older, and this vestibular incident really brought this to the forefront of my attention. I noticed more of the grey and white furs on her face and around her muzzle. Luna started to bring this to my attention more and more. Reminders of how precious time and moments are with the ones we love and that each day is a treasure to be embraced and enjoyed. Luna was the jewel of my heart. She always shined so much light, love, laughter, and brightness to my world and to my every day. She was also like a flower to me, as she was always open in full bloom and full of life, love, joy, and wisdom. So, we treasured every moment even more. It seemed as though time passed by so quickly.

I was so grateful as Luna reminded me about following my heart and my intuition. In many ways, she was my compass of direction in following all that I was guided to. She also reminded me that the guidance of your heart, your truth, and the pulls and tugs of your heartstrings are what bring the most joy. She also reminded me of following your own path and trusting in yourself, your inner guidance, and your heart, as your heart always knows.

The months passed, and before I knew it, it was December. Luna had developed an ear hematoma. This was not the first experience with her having an ear hematoma. The first had been several years prior, and it had required surgery. I woke up with Luna beside me, with her head on the pillow next to me. The interesting thing was she looked at me with a steadfast stare, letting me know something was wrong. She guided me to her left ear, and it was all filled up like a water balloon, and her other ear was completely flat. I thought to myself, *How on earth did this happen?* So, off to the emergency vet we went, where Luna was diagnosed with an ear hematoma caused by shaking her head from having an ear infection. It could have been drained, but with no guarantee that it would get rid of all the fluid. So, surgery was the only option as her ear was completely filled up with fluid. Oh my—not what I had planned for at that moment. Sometimes you just have to find a way to make things happen and know that it all will work itself out somehow. The vet said she would need the surgery right away, so I reached out to friends to see what experience they'd had with hematomas. I also called Luna's regular vet, as I was more comfortable having them do the surgery. She was able to get in that week, and they even helped work it out so I could drop her off the night before surgery, as I had to work early the next morning. The house was very empty that night without Luna.

It was so hard to work the next morning, as all I could think about was Luna, but it was also a good distraction. She ended up doing well in surgery, and I could hardly wait to get off work and go pick her up. The end of the day came, and off I was to pick up my girl and a happy reunion it was. The vet went over all the care instructions with me. Her ear looked like a dot-to-dot drawing of constellations. To see what they did to get rid of the hematoma was fascinating to me. Luna did not share my same fascination, although she did feel relief from having the hematoma drained and prepped for the healing to begin. The cone of shame was there to help with the healing process. I know Luna was less than thrilled about that part.

So, home we went, where Linnus and Leo were wondering what was going on with Luna and why she smelled so weird— you know, all animals know that unmistakable vet office smell. Nonetheless, they were still happy to see her back home. The vet had prescribed pain medication for her, which ended up not really helping Luna, as it made her out of sorts. She was whining and crying, which was very out of character for her. It broke my heart to see her this way. I was supposed to go to work, but I was not about to leave my Luna at home all out of sorts. I called into work and made an appointment for Luna to go into the vet to make sure all was well with her. It turned out it was her recovering from the surgery, and this was a slight reaction to the pain medication. So, the necessary adjustments were made, and Luna ended up healing well.

The time came for the stitches to be removed. I made sure they did it in the exam room, as it was fascinating to me to see how the dot to dot in her ear was going to be revealed. This hematoma was a reminder to be more diligent with weekly ear cleaning, as one shake of her head too hard could be the breeding ground and cause for unwanted hematomas. She went many years without a hematoma until a small one developed in her other ear. Off to the vet, we went. The good news is that this time it was a small enough hematoma to be drained without surgery. Luckily, the vet was able to drain it while I was in the room with Luna, add some medication, wrap it up, and provide some medication to help with the healing. As it healed, I had to change the bandage and add medication every day. We really dodged a bullet as it ended up healing up completely.

Now back to December, when her third hematoma came, which I know now was part of a bigger underlying issue that needed to be brought to my attention. The thing is, we had yet to establish care with a new vet. Thank goodness for Facebook, as I had been seeing an ad for a vet in the area where we were now living. I was able to get her in for an appointment to have the hematoma looked at, and it ended up being another small one. Luna was older now, about 14, and surgery to drain it was not really the option I was looking for. While we were there, I was able to have a couple of lumps looked at. One the vet was not as concerned with due to the way it felt and moved, so it was more due to her age and breed. The other one, however, was on her back by her right hip. It was the size of a golf ball, did not really have any movement, and was a harder lump. A needle aspirate was needed to take some fluid out of it to see if it had cancer cells in it. They drained her ear, provided medication, and did the needle aspirate. I hoped for the best with both. The vet let me know the fluid that was drawn from the lump would have to be sent out for further testing. I knew something was wrong. I tried my best to remain positive as Luna had been the most stable, consistent presence in my life since the moment she came into it. She was my world, my best friend, my heart, the absolute love and light of my life and every day. It was going to take a few days to get the results back. The day the phone rang, I was not looking forward to the call. The vet let me know the results were back and confirmed my Luna had cancer—she was diagnosed with a soft tissue sarcoma.

Thankfully, I was at home when I got the call. I remember as soon as I heard those words, I dropped to my knees as tears ran down my face, as hysteria filled every part of me. I looked at my girl, and she reminded me of all we had shared and that we would get through this together. The vet was so kind, calm, and empathetic and knew just what I needed to hear. She went over what type of cells of cancer it was, and I shook as I wrote down notes. Options of what to do were discussed of having the tumor removed. It also turned out that at the same time, the hematoma had come back, and options of what to do for that were discussed. It was as though my whole world was crashing down in front of me and before my eyes. So much to think about and to figure out. We worked together in coming up with a plan that honored her wishes. Five months prior, the vestibular incident that had come up had helped me to prepare for the fact that her time on the physical plane was limited. It was also four months prior that we had that final trip to the coast, and now I know why that trip was so important for my Luna and me. Here I was in December, just like when I got Linnus's cancer diagnosis.

Many pet owners arrive at this time when a beloved animal is diagnosed in this way. It is an important time to really listen to one's animal companion. Luna started to show me signs when I was not in her physical presence that ultimately helped me to know that our relationship was tangible even when we were not together physically. This helped me prepare for her passing. One of the most important things that came to me was to honor Luna's wishes, as it was not about me and my wishes; it was about her, her body, and how she was feeling. It was important to honor her desires.

I also ended up talking with the vet who saw the tumor to get more perspective. She was truly kind and compassionate. I felt so grateful for those two vets, as they both were so receptive to my thoughts and questions without passing any judgments. In my gut, I just knew I could not put my Luna through surgery. Tuning in to her, she conveyed to me she just wanted to enjoy the time she had left, and she and her body did not want to go through surgery. Especially when there was no guarantee of the outcome. The vet said the hematoma could change the shape of her ear without surgery, as draining it again was not really going to be a viable option. The thing is, it didn't fill up all the way again—it was pretty small, and Luna did not want it messed with as she let me know the cancer was not allowing it to completely resolve itself, and she was okay with that.

This was a hard one for me as I always did everything I could for my girl and her well-being. The thought of judgment from others rushed through my head. Luna let me know it is not for others to judge; it is between her and me, and more importantly, honoring her wishes was what was most important. This was an enormously powerful lesson from her to me. I had to not only work through the judgment of others, but I had to also work with the judgment I was putting on myself. Luna helped me with this. She communicated this message to me:

> *Despite of my cancer, I'm not my cancer. I'm my soul filled with love and wisdom for you. For the bubbles and springs of my love are always with you and in your heart. Our love is strong, one in a million, reaching beyond the stars and beyond time. It blossoms always. I am me, the love of your heart, the depths of your truth, the seeker of your word, and your passion for the animals. I will always be your girl throughout time, for time is just time. And love is always love and will always be. The light of me shines in you always. The beacon of your light will always shine, and I will always be there shining on with you. It is about being our best even when our faith is tested. These tests are part of our journey, and when one end happens, another one begins like the waves flood through the tides of change. Just be joy, because "what is" is not a defining factor of*

*you, because cancer sucks ass big time. But I am still your
tough persnickety girl, and I will fight to the end and not
let it get me down. So, mom, enjoy what we have now for
it's precious, and know how much I love you. Shine,
sparkle, and be the best you can be, like what you are and
have been for me. Cherish the flame and feel my love
rolling in you because when you need that kick, I'm forever
always your girl. Your Lunabe.*

Luna's and my plan was to enjoy the time we had and to
give her comfort, and watch the tumor's growth. So, knowing
this was going to be Luna's last Christmas, I made sure to go
all out for her. She had a variety of treats and toys, and of
course, Leo had presents too. Luna also had a very special
Christmas dinner. I went off to the store to look at options for
her Christmas feast. I looked at steaks and roast. I remembered
how much Luna enjoyed roast when we were staying with my
parents, as my mom would usually share a tiny piece with her.
I knew that was a treat for Luna, as I never cooked red meat.
So, she savored the smell and taste when she could. The
thought that came to me was that a roast would be perfect. So,
a roast is what I was in search of, and I found the perfect one.
No roast is complete without carrots and potatoes, so of course,
I made sure those were also in my cart. Luckily, Luna was not
picky, as I ended up cooking the roast a little too long. Guess
that's what happens when it's not something you usually cook.
Luna was so excited that this was all for her. She did let Leo
have a couple of little pieces. She loved it, and she had a special
treat for a few days.

Due to the weather, we were not able to travel to my parents' for Christmas that year. So, it was a quiet Christmas at home with my Luna and Leo. And the snow, which Luna loved. It made me so happy to see how much she was able to enjoy the snow. She would roll all about in it and just enjoy laying in it until it turned icier and less slushy. We enjoyed time frolicking in it together, a reminder of how simple joys in life bring smiles to our hearts. We had many great times in the snow, and I have many great pictures and videos with Luna in it, and of Luna and I in the snow together. It warms my heart to look at these videos and pictures. It also reminds me there are pictures that we capture with our hearts. Then, there are pictures we capture that bring moments to our hearts and minds. These memories are there to bring us peace, comfort, and joy. They remind us that love always remains, as do the memories of that love. That we can easily tap into that energy, and that it is always within our reach to share the joy of those memories, which is the treasure of all treasures.

That Christmas was one of my favorite Christmases, as it was filled with my Luna and Leo, and was a day of enjoying time together. Of course, it was hard not to be able to go see my parents, but I now realize the importance of that Christmas with my babies. Luna was not much of a dog that was fond of dog toys. Sure, she enjoyed them from time to time. One of her favorite types of toys was any kind of rope toy. The toys most dogs enjoyed, she was not fond of. There was one toy that was different than most. It was not only a special toy to her; it was also a special toy to me. This was one of her Christmas toys from what would be our last Christmas together. It happened to be a stuffed reindeer. The most amazing thing was the fact that this particular toy was still pretty much intact, aside from a small piece missing from its neck about the size of a dime, which was quite amazing because Luna would usually destroy toys like this in no time flat. It was as though she knew to keep this toy intact, as it would bring me much comfort after she passed. On her last days, we played many games of tug-tug with this toy. I captured some video of Luna making her special *grr grr* sound while we were playing the tug-tug game. I used to call it her Luna sound. I have this toy tucked away in a special place, and it is there as a reminder that her comfort is always there with me. This reindeer shows me that in a tangible way so I can connect to that comfort. In this moment, she reminded me that my connection to her is always there. It is just a matter of tuning into the comfort of her connection.

Luna began to walk more quietly on our last walks together; the beautiful sway in her walk she once had was no longer noticeable. It was even apparent on our shorter walks to the trash can, and I could feel her pain and slowing down. As much as she wanted to stay with me, her body was becoming weak, while other outer appearances seemed to be normal, the status quo. I knew by listening to her using my feelers with our connection that her time on the earth's physical plane was coming to an end. The light in her eyes grew diminished, was not as bright, as though part of her essence was in a different space of time and existence. Like she was there, but not all there, as she would just have these blank stares on her face.

Luna and I treasured the final time we had with each other. It was about being in the moments together, not about how many moments we had left, and instead, enjoying the ones we did. I often would put my hand in her paw, she would nestle her head in my armpit, we would share Eskimo kisses, as they were the one silly thing Luna indulged and humored me with. In her final week, I painted a heart dish that is full of color; it reminds me of the vibrancy of our love and the strength of it. The cremation place gave me a heart print mold of her paw, and it brings me much peace, as it did to Leo, who used to set his paws on it. I also have some of her fur, which gives me strength, and the box containing her ashes sits on my table with other memories of her. Leo, from time to time, will rub on it for comfort from his Luna.

I also made my own paw print art of Luna. It did not turn out as well as I had hoped, and its imperfection is a reminder of the imperfect times Luna helped me through and that she will always continue to help me through those times. On Facebook, I had seen how people were making paw print art as memorials for their pets. One would use different color watercolors and dip their pets' paw in there and then put it on paper. The idea behind this was to have the paw print be in the shape of a flower. I thought to myself, *What a perfectly grand idea.* Well, Luna was not so inclined as to think this was a grand idea. I remember explaining to her how fun and cool this was going to be. So, the fun began, where I said, "Luna let me take your paw and put it in the paint, then on the paper." With a total look of disapproval on her face, she complied, as she knew it was important to me. Oh my, how that look increased when I dipped her paw in the water to clean it for the next color. She looked at me as though she had been completely violated. She knew this was important to me, so she just insisted I be quick about it and not dilly dally. They did not turn out the way I anticipated them to, but they turned out just as they were supposed to—a reminder of this experience with my Luna. She reminded me again that not everything is perfect and that is okay.

Luna knew how hard it was going to be for me to not have her physical presence in my life. She helped orchestrate this transition not only for me, but for her and for her Leo. When I found out about her cancer diagnosis, I started to look online and in-person at local Humane Societies to keep my eye out for what kind of dogs were out there. Sure, I had in mind the kind of dog I was looking for. I soon found out it doesn't always work out this way. I knew the time was coming near for me to make one of hardest and most heart-wrenching decisions of my life, it was not only a decision for me, but it also had to be in Luna's best interest. About a month prior, I had a quality of life appointment with the vet. How was I to face this and make this choice?

That week I happened to be at the Humane Society and encountered the most beautiful dog. Her name was Kulap, and she was a shepherd/spaniel mix. I thought to myself, *I never imagined having a dog like this in my life.* There was something that pulled me to her—a connection I felt. I went home and could not get her out of my mind. I kept looking at her picture on their website. She was on my mind the next day too, which happened to be the day I knew I had to make the appointment for Luna's transition. I called the vet and had set the appointment up for that Friday. The next day, I went back to the

Humane Society, and she was still there; my heart had almost jumped out of my chest in relief. The only thing was is that there was another family that had put a hold on her. They mentioned I could put a second hold on her and asked if I would like to officially meet her and do that. I said sure, and wondered what had come over me, and how crazy this was, but I just went with it. I fell in love with her sweetness and a little bit of sass. The next thing I knew, I was putting the $15 hold fee down for her. I just let it go and knew if it were meant to be, it would be.

On Friday afternoon, I had the appointment for Luna set up that evening. The phone rang, I missed the call, and soon there was a message from the Humane Society to call them back. So, of course, I called them back straight away. They were calling to let me know the other hold had backed out and that I had 24 hours to decide if I wanted to adopt Kulap, as someone else had put a hold on her after me. Of course, I said yes and let them know I would be in the next day to adopt her. Crazy right? It felt right, and happiness and tears overcame me. I knew Luna wanted to make sure Leo and I were not alone, and she was not able to leave until she knew that. There was no doubt in my mind that this was meant to be with how it aligned just so. Luna wanted to make sure I had the love, joy and comfort from another dog, so she knew I would not be without the physical presence of the love of a dog in my life.

The time to take Luna to the vet had arrived. I tried to get her to give me one last howl before we left, but she was not having it. Instead, she grabbed her reindeer toy, shook it about and had me play tug-tug with her as she wanted me to feel joy from the beautiful moments we shared together. I gathered her and Leo up as I wanted to make sure Leo was a part of the process, as they had an unbreakable bond. I knew how important it was for him to have closure too. We had one stop to make before the vet, and it was to McDonald's for one big treat. Luna enjoyed a plain double cheeseburger, fries, and of course, an apple pie for dessert.

My heart felt so empty and sad when we pulled up to the vet. They had a room ready for us. They made sure to give me time before giving Luna the medication that would make her tired. The time came, and I was there holding her the whole time. She passed peacefully. Leo came to say his goodbye and gave her a final look over. I just sat with her, cuddling and laying with her, as I did not want to let go of her touch, strength, or her energy. It was time to make the drive back home, and tears filled every part of me. At a stoplight, in the clouds, a rainbow appeared out of the blue to give me comfort, and the song *Just like Heaven* by Bryan Adams came on. We had arrived home, and the house was so empty without Luna. Leo and I curled up together to give each other comfort. The next day, the sun rose, and emptiness was in the air. Then came the time to get Kulap and bring her home, and the house filled up with joy again. For Luna would not have it any other way. Luna was and will always be my greatest teacher!

What matters most in life is the love we share and give and how it impacts our life. What truly matters is how we feel our thoughts—we vibrate out through the hemisphere as these thoughts spiral out into the universe. Be love, feel love, be all you can be. Be happy with being all you can be, for your worth is truly yours to determine. It's not about what others think and say, it's about what you see and feel with your heart and all you are. For it is the things we feel within the depths of our hearts that are truly powerful, as it is a direct connection with our soul and all we can be. So, give yourself—not time to think—instead, give yourself time to *feel* beyond the staircase of your heart within the depths of who you truly are and what you are truly capable of. Feel and see with your heart's eye.

Luna also reminded me that, even though sometimes things happen in certain months, it does not mean those months are bad, that it can be a time of gratitude for the memories that come up. This was especially helpful for me in the month of December, as that is when Linnus passed away from cancer. Then two years later is when I received Luna's cancer diagnosis in December of 2016, and she passed away on March 3, 2017. It was in December of 2019 that Leo's health declined, and it was most likely cancer, based on test results. I had made the hard decision to help Leo transition on December 22, 2019, which was just one day before Linnus had passed four years earlier on Winter Solstice, December 21, 2015. It is so interesting that the timing of each diagnosis was in December, and that they had all passed about two years apart from each other. It was almost as though they had some sort of pact, my little trio of love, light, goodness, and wisdom they were. Leo also shared much wisdom with me, especially with how important animal communication is and how important it is to listen to what they speak and communicate to us. One of the most profound pieces of wisdom came from Leo when I held him up to a mirror that we both gazed into. What he communicated to me was: "I don't have to look in the mirror to know I'm beautiful." Wow, what insight and clarity that brought me to remember to love all of me—what is on the outside and on the inside.

Luna enjoying a nice soak in the water in Cannon Beach,
Oregon on our trip for my Birthday August13, 2016.

Chapter Ten

THE END IS
ANOTHER BEGINNING

Life after Luna's passing was not easy. One thing that helps me is the many ways she is even more of a presence in my life. Luna helped Leo and me heal after she passed. She has sent me many signs since she passed, and I know these signs are from her. There are many ways to identify signs one is receiving from their soulmate animal, as one feels it within the depths of their heart. After she passed, Luna often reminded me through gentle reminders and memories how precious life was with her and how much we enjoyed the last bit of borrowed time we had together. One of the most profound messages she conveyed to me was, "Happiness is a gift to be treasured and enjoyed." I took this to mean for me to dig into those memories and happy times that we had together.

I met Kulap the week Luna passed, and both she and Kulap helped me to prepare to say goodbye to Luna. Luna wanted to make sure I would not be without the physical presence of the love of a dog in my life. Some people judged me for getting another dog so soon. Luna helped me process this, and I now share this wisdom with clients as they deal with a beloved pet's passing. I can help them move beyond the judgment of others. Luna helped Kulap and I adjust to our new life together. I remember that one of the first times I had to leave Kulap alone in her kennel, I called in the presence of Luna and could feel her energy lay right in front of Kulap's kennel to offer her comfort and security. There was even one time when Kulap came up to my bed and started rolling on it, and I could feel Luna's essence coming through Kulap at that moment.

After Luna passed, I intuitively knew I needed to keep searching for my biological father. I had always thought about trying Ancestory.com, but I was never brave enough to follow through, not knowing what the results would yield. For my birthday, my parents got me an Ancestory.com DNA test. What a great and thoughtful gift this was! I was so nervous about doing the test and about sending off the results. I finally mustered up the courage to send off my test. This was about eighteen months after Luna passed, and I found out my biological father had passed about a decade earlier. The journey I made with Luna, one of connection and then loss, helped me deal with the fact that I never got to meet him while he was on the physical plane. Instead, we have a different kind of connection, as I know he is one of my guides. Learning his name and seeing his picture for the first time gave me a deep feeling of peace and completion. I had always been curious, but never realized how important knowing who he was meant to me. I was happy to know who he was, yet there were so many unanswered questions about *who* he was. My heart feels full by knowing who he was, but empty for not having met him in the physical world. The connection I have made with this side of my biological family and the wholeness this has brought to my life is the greatest gift Luna gave me.

One of the signs that came to me after Luna passed came in the form of a semi-truck, which is remarkably interesting if you think about it. I was driving and saw a semi-truck that said Heartland Express on it. Mind you, I have never seen this semi-truck before Luna's passing. In between the words was a heart on the driver's door, and on the truck, the words Heartland Express with a heart with what looked like wings on either side of the heart. What a perfect sign from my heart dog! A message that our hearts are always connected and, with what looked like wings, showing that she is always there looking over me. I periodically still see this truck, always when I need to see it most. I never saw this truck until after Luna's passing. One time right after seeing this truck, I heard *You'll Be in My Heart* by Phil Collins come on my radio, which was a sure sign to me that this was from my girl. She also comes to me in license plates that have "bea" or "be" in them, as one of my favorite nicknames for her was Luna Bea or Bee, and it was always one of her favorites as well. So, I know without a doubt when I see a license plate that has this in it, and I think of her, that she is also thinking of me and sending her love to me from the heavens. To me, this is a reminder that our beloveds orchestrate ways for us to know that their presence is always with us, just sometimes in a different way than it was before, a different kind of tangible, the kind we feel with our heart's eye.

Also, pay attention to other animals in your household, as they are very easily in tune with the energy around them. As my Leo has reminded me, he might just be sitting or lying down staring off at a wall, and when I acknowledge that it is Luna, he shifts his focus ever-so-slightly to let me know it is, in fact, her. This gives us both peace and comfort. Luna has also come to me in the sign of a crow, which is very symbolic to me, as it shows her wisdom for me is continued on the other side. You may ask how I know this is her, but the question to me is, how can I not know? It is a feeling that comes in as a very subtle awareness and there is no denying it. Let me re-phrase that. We may, as humans in our logical mind, try to deny it, as it comes with such ease and flow that we doubt it. This is a reminder that things do not have to be as complicated as we sometimes make them. A reminder that the things that live within our hearts are always pure and there for us to connect to with ease and flow. I invite you to be open to these signs and to let them flow to you with ease. A new awareness of ease will fill every ounce of your heart with happiness and the remainder of the heartfelt connection that always remains and is constantly stirring within us.

Another sign from Luna came to me while visiting my parents. I was out in their front yard, which was always one of Luna's favorite places. I was really craving and wanting a sign from her. So, I asked her to show me a sign. Suddenly, a wind chime attached to a gate at the end of the front yard started to move. Then it stopped, and I asked Luna, is that you? Within the next moment, it started to move again. So, the reason I share this with you is a reminder that you can call in the energy of the presence of loved ones that have passed away. It is as simple as it sounds. I invite you to give it a try; those you love are there to support you and remind you of their love. They are also always there cheering us on and supporting us. They offer subtle ways of reminding us of their presence. Just be open with no expectations, and I guarantee you will be amazed, as you will realize the signs you have been feeling and experiencing without having been aware of them.

On March 3, 2018, it had been one year since Luna passed, and I was thinking how I wished I could see my girl that morning on my way to work. Then, I was drawn to the clouds, where I saw an image of her sitting there and sending her love and presence down to me. This moment reminded me of something I saw the month I had gotten her cancer diagnosis. I had been out doing some shopping and was drawn to a jacket that said, "Never look back," and I knew that Luna wanted me to not look back on whether there was something I could have done differently to have discovered her cancer earlier. What was important was to focus on the now moment and time we had left together. Signs she gave me like this before she passed and feeling her presence behind me holding me up in strength now reminds me that she is more a part of me now—intertwined with my soul, a new linking since she passed.

I always love to mix it up and change the background on my phone. After Luna passed, I found a beautiful image of a beautiful pure blue sky with some clouds and a profound heart cloud in the center of the sky. I always loved looking at this image and was so captivated by it. One day, looking in it, I saw Luna's image sitting there in the clouds, which reminded me that her strength and love were always surrounding me. Years prior to Luna's passing, I purchased a dog figurine on a trip to Iowa because I was drawn to it, as it reminded me of my girl. I now call it my Luna dog figurine, as her spirit comes through there, which reminds me her essence is always there and can be called in at any time, at any given moment.

Luna had me channel a message from her on 10/1/17, a few months after her passing. The message from her was as follows:

> *You were there with me when I started to fade; you felt my energy slide in and out like the slider on a fader. Moving in and out, fading further away from you physically, yet closer to you spiritually. Closer to the center of your heartstrings, intertwining more into your soul for the deeper work that comes into play for us now. You can see it in my eyes in the picture of us on our last trip to the coast, the blank stare and heartbreak in my eyes knowing I didn't have long with you left in this lifetime, although I still had time with you in a different way. I will always be your strength, your grounding angel pushing you to the next heights of existence. For although my physical existence is not with you, it is embedded in your heart and soul and is even stronger now. How can that be possible, for me to be physically more with you when I am not physically with you? How is that, you ask? It is the fact that the physical strain of my body is not pulling me away from you. As I am more present now in the light of the heavens, the light that comes through the pictures in the sun with you and Kulap. For I sent her to you before my passing to give you a distraction. For you to have her*

*presence to help heal your heart and give you the love that
you shared with me. I still send you signs from me and my
wisdom and will always be the keeper of your heart.
Remember me and my steadfast wonder of strength. And
Linnus says he sends you grounding in your knowledge at
your feet and at your fingertips. Love, love, love, and give
my Leo a kiss for me!! That's all for now.*

One of the greatest bits of wisdom Luna gave me was,
"Don't pant your way through life; soar to new heights and
reach for the sky of new possibilities!" This wisdom has been a
great reminder for me and one I remember to follow to this
day. Another wisdom Luna gave me that aligns with this one
is, "Just don't scratch the surface, for you want to dig deep."
I'm so grateful for all the wisdom she shared with me during
her life and the wisdom she continues to light my way with.
Luna always humored me and inspired me, and that impact
she had on me still carries on as she helped me to see how doing
things that might be out of our comfort zone can bring profound inspirations. Luna reminded me that we can make the
intangible tangible, and that sometimes it is about seeing with
our heart's eyes, as well as holding the vision in our minds.

Luna continues to remind me of how important it is to
soak in time with those that are near and dear to your heart.
She still shows me how significant our last trip to the coast
together was and the memories that it holds that are locked
inside my heart. It is now why I soak in special moments like
the ones I had with Luna, as our connection is one I never

experienced on such deep levels with any other soul the way I did with her. I'm forever grateful for my soulmate dog, Luna, and the piece of home that is her and is locked in love, light and wisdom in my heart. Remember to laugh, have fun, let go, be free, know how precious life is, enjoy every moment. Take time for today instead of worrying about yesterday and tomorrow.

*Luna and I on our last trip together to Cannon Beach,
Oregon on August 13, 2016.*

ABOUT THE AUTHOR

Shawna Fischer is a charismatic animal communicator based in Vancouver, Washington. Since a young age, she has been communicating with animals and has always found comfort in their presence. She had no idea how deep that communication could be until a feisty and wise yellow lab named Luna came into her life. Excited by the possibility to use her innate gift to bring comfort to both animals and their people, Shawna started to read as much as she could on the subject. She took classes with Marta Williams in California and Amelia Kinkade in Federal Way, Washington, and started practicing animal communication on a more regular basis. In 2011 she launched her business, and her website: www.shawnamariefischer.com. She has been practicing animal communication professionally for about ten years. She has been interviewed on radio shows, hosted her own internet radio show, and was a co-host on an additional radio show. She has taught classes online and in person. Her passion is helping humans deepen their connection with their animals. Shawna lives with her Australian Shepherd-Spaniel-mix, Kulap, her Golden Retriever-mix Nugget, and her Tuxedo cat, Mojo.

Continue the Journey with Me

Continue the journey with me by setting up a session with connecting you to the deeper innerworkings of your soulmate animal. I work with clients all over the world via Zoom or phone, and offer 60-minute or 90-minute sessions. Whether you are wanting more insight into something that is going on with an animal in your life, be it a behavior issue, medical issue, or an end of life decision, or if you are wanting help in healing from the loss of one of your soulmate animals that has crossed the rainbow bridge, I can help bring messages from your beloved pet to bring you peace through their love.

To schedule a session, please visit my website:

shawnamariefischer.com.

If you have any questions, please feel free to email me at: shawna@shawnamariefischer.com. I'd love to hear from you.

You can also connect with me on social media:

YouTube:
www.youtube.com/channel/UCZ2wZqSWaXGF2trZjMHo
O1g

Facebook:
www.facebook.com/fischershawnamarie

Instagram:
www.instagram.com/shawnamariefischer/

Bonus Gift

As a bonus gift for my readers, please enjoy this free meditation download:

Meditation Journey with Your Soulmate Animal

This meditation will help you continue the journey into unlocking wisdom from your soulmate, connecting with parts of your journey together.

Download it here:

shawnamariefischer.com/bonus-meditation

ACKNOWLEDGMENTS

With extreme gratitude to my parents that raised me, for I would not be who I am today without their unconditional love and support.

Thank you to my biological parents that brought me into this world.

Of course, I'd like to thank Luna for this book and the home I found within myself that would have not been possible without her.

In gratitude to Luna's foster mom for bringing Luna into my world.

Julie, thank you for your unending support as I put together this book. I'm grateful for you.

Thank you to Lisa Fugard for helping with my book proposal and for helping me uncover more of my writing for this book.

A heartfelt thank you to Sunny Dawn Johnston and her amazing team for cheering me on during the writing process.

Thank you to Shanda Trofe and her amazing team at Transcendent Publishing for helping my book shine.

I'm grateful to Kyra and Todd Schaefer for helping me with getting my book together.

I'm grateful for all my wonderful friends and family for their support.

Last but not least, thank you to all my fabulous clients and their animals, and the inspiration they bring into my life.

CPSIA information can be obtained
at www.ICGtesting.com
Printed in the USA
JSHW030629180222
22959JS00003B/15